Flowers
&
Tightropes

by Katie Bainbridge

About the Author

Katie Bainbridge has been a jack-of-all-trades and is now a mistress of her own destiny, working as a writer and an administrator for a UK charity. Katie lives in Cornwall with her flatmate and friend, Anja, and also her beloved kitty cat, Izzy.

Copyright
Samphira Books

Names have been changed and/or omitted to protect identities.

Copyright © Katie Bainbridge 2015

All rights reserved. No part of this publication may be reproduced, stored in a retrieval system, or transmitted, in any form or by any means without the prior consent of the publisher.

The publisher is not responsible for websites (addresses given in this book), their content or links that are not owned by the publisher.

To contact Samphira Books regarding this publication, please email: samphirakatie@gmail.com

Cover artwork by 'covermaestro' at Fiverr

Book titles by
Katie Bainbridge include:

The Book of Mirrors 2009 (Paperback) & ebook 2016
The Book of Windows 2010 (Paperback) & ebook 2016
The Book of Dark Stories (E-book) 2016
Flowers & Tightropes 2015 (E-book)

Contents

Acknowledgements ix
Introduction xi

Part One
Tightropes

The Days of Magic & Wonder 1
Growing Pains 5
Magic & Mayhem 8
The Big, Bad World! 10
Life (As I Knew It) – Poem 13
On Being A Man 15
Eczema – A Living Hell 17
The Edge of The Wilderness 20
My Descent Into Madness 23
Out of The Wilderness 25
Still Crazy But Safe 26
Finding My Wings – Meeting Susan 29
Leaving Susan 31
Lies & Doctors 33
Kinks 35
Have It Their Way – Poem 38
Have It Your Way – Poem 39
Dirty Drugs & Incompetence 40

Unhealthy Expectations 41
Where I Am Now 43

Part Two
Flowers

Life In General 51
Victims 54
A Hidden Blessing 56
A list Of Crap Things To Say 57
'Cause Ah's Black, Innit?! 60
A Cure For Prejudice 62
A Slightly Alternative Look at Prejudice, I Think 64
The Gender Trap 68
Doing The Best We Can 71
Inner Conflict 73
The Committing Of Sin – Poem 75
Sexual Shame 77
Going To The Toilet 78
Small-mindedness 80
Body Shame 82
Male Or Female – What Are They? 85
More of the Mystery Unravels! 87
Seeking Refuge 89
Our History 92
The Shop – Poem 94

Being Different	96
Too Shy?	98
Assumptions	100
L.G.B.T Wot?! - Poem	102
Femisism is Still a Great Word	103
Drummer Statue, Truro	105
I Had A Dream – Poem	106
Jesus Wept!	107
Dying For Our Beliefs – Poem	108
Hall Of Mirrors – Poem	109
Questions	110
Cornwall Pride	111
Addendum	113

Acknowledgements

I would like to thank my mother for her ongoing support of me. I would also like to thank my friend Anja Kersten, without whom I would have got lost a long time ago, regarding the writing of this book. You can't beat having a creative coach (just one of her incarnations) as a flatmate! My firm belief still stands that those who enter our lives do so for a purpose and those people are our mirrors.

Last and by no means least, my little furry companion whom I would not be without; Izzy. My gentle, loyal and loving cat baby.

Introduction

This book is about my journey from male to female. No, wait! Hang on just one minute because I'm not entirely sure that is the truth. No! I believe that this book is about my journey from Eddie to Katie and a return to me. I was always female inside, no matter what my external features were and this is something that I hope comes over to the reader of my book. If it were possible to transplant the essence of 'Me' into the body of a parrot, I would still be Katie. I may now have the body of a parrot but it would not change the fact of who I am inside.

I also wish to enlighten the reader about our sense of identity and how, as a society, we seem to have lost a lot of respect for each other's spiritual and emotional identity. I want to bring awareness to the fact of how we shoe-horn each other into boxes that do not fit who we are and then expect that person to be okay with it. After cramming a limitless potential into a space no bigger than the person we perceive, we then expect that person to grow up into a fully functional and rounded human being. Not at all possible! I will take you on a journey that will hopefully let you see that growing into who we really are could be an exciting and joyous time, instead of one filled with fear and shame.

If this book saves anyone even a quarter of the pain that I have been through, then it will have been more than worthwhile. This book is as individual and quirky as I am. It has all the strangeness and uniqueness that I possess. At the same time, if you are honest with yourself when reading it, there will be much that you can identify with, whether you label yourself as transgender or not. *Flowers & Tightropes* is written in two parts. The first part is *Tightropes* – my life story. The second part is *Flowers* – the insights that I have gained from my life.

Part One

Tightropes

The Days of Magic & Wonder

My short time in Scotland was a memorable one. I loved where I lived and the countryside around. It was full of magic. I don't care what people say; there really are elves, fairies and water spirits! I have been fortunate enough to see them. I believe that science, in its own plodding, laborious way, will one day discover this realm and hopefully before it's too late.

I cannot express in words the joy I had just visiting the glen and going for walks with my Grandma. Pure magic! I always got so excited about going out for walks too (I'm beginning to sound like a dog). It was a new adventure each time. If only life still had that feeling. It does some days but I get caught up in the mundane too often and forget its mystery and potential for discovery. Here is a poem I wrote about my walks with Grandma:

Days To Remember

Of all the things I remember most
I remember the country walks,
Just Gran and me and fields and trees
And our wonderful little talks.

We always passed by Mr Muir's
(Though Mr Manure to myself),
And further on was a bubbling spring
Where I swore there lived an elf!

I'll always remember that little spring
That bubbled from a rock,
An arched and stony temple
With fern and moss and dock.

On the right beyond the spring
Was a road up to the dam,
Where Gran and I would skim flat stones
On its waters still and calm.

Now, at the dam was a strange old hut
With both its green doors padlocked shut,
And from within those flushing sounds
And always just so 'out of bounds'.

I shoved those doors an inch at most
Then tried the keyhole as a spy-let,
I decided it must be a ghost
Doomed forever to use the toilet!

And on we'd go to The Magic Glen
If ever was one this was!
Secluded, lush, with crystal pools
In silence we would pause.

I remember its mossy, earthy smells
And how my gran would fret,
As I got close to the water's edge
And always ended up wet!

What joy to live a life so free
What did we do to merit,
A place so full of love and grace
That each step was taken in spirit?

Days out with Mum were always special too. I was more than happy to tag along wherever she wanted go. I loved a good look around Stirling and its shops, going for an ice cream, the simple things. We would sometimes go and visit Grandma where she worked. Grandma was very clever with numbers and she worked in the accounts department of a department store.

My playmate that lived down the road was a good friend to me. I can vividly remember us standing on the garage roof with newspapers tied to our arms, trying to fly. We had a play shed at the top of my garden that had a car battery and a car headlight tied to the roof for lighting. My dad made a hole in the back of the shed, put in a tap and rigged up a one gallon water container that one pumped up to get pressure, and that provided running water. It was really a pesticide sprayer that was bought solely for this purpose and never used as intended.

I will never forget that sense of impending discovery with everything. I had a joy that I plumb my depths to rediscover every now and then but, back then, it was quite a usual thing. I know things weren't perfect when I lived in Scotland and, even as a child my health was often not too good, but there was magic and awe in my life. Nothing is as precious as that!

I had three main friends that I would play with out of school. They were Colin, Graham and, of course, Julie who lived in the next house down the road. It was a rounded bunch of friends. Colin liked to build houses with me in the massive sand pit I had or make waterways in it with an old barrel of water at the top. Graham used to like building bonfires which I also loved. Julie and I were obsessed with trying to fly, playing at shops and houses, building dens and generally being quite inventive with things. I loved playing shops and playing with my treasure trove of foreign coins and notes. We also used to love imagining there was treasure to find and used to dig holes everywhere in the garden, much to Mum's dismay sometimes! They were good days in many respects. I have fond memories.

Growing Pains

School life for me was, as the Americans so beautifully put it, an 'epic fail'. I had two good years to begin with at a quite exclusive private school in Scotland. I shall never forget those two years as they were, in many ways, a saviour to me; a rock of school sanity in a very messed up career.

When did you become transgender? some people ask me. I reply, I didn't become, I always was transgender. I was born this way. That was what made life at school so bloody awful. I was a very sensitive and emotional girl masquerading around as a boy! I'll say one thing though, it taught me how boys/men treat each other and it's totally shit. No wonder a lot of men can't express their feelings. They're too frightened to, probably. No, you couldn't pay me enough money or give any reward big enough to make me voluntarily 'be a man'.

So, to school and my hellish journey through 'the system'.
As I said earlier, it started off well. These were the best two years of my school career. I was taught and got respect. We were allowed to express ourselves and give opinions, weren't judged about being too male or female and religion wasn't rammed down our throats although we sang hymns in assembly which I loved.

I noticed even then that I was different, or at least felt it. I loved to play with the girls, and the boys too, but there was a difference I didn't notice that was pointed out to me, and that was that I 'shouldn't have a favourite boy'. I loved to mix with both sexes as the games they played differed so much. Some were rough and tumble and others were homemaking and tea parties or dressing up; something I definitely was not encouraged to do by the boys!

I began to flourish at this school. Begin was all that I was going to do though and who can say what would have become of me had I stayed on. On the 1st November 1975, we moved to England. Not a great move in many ways. Not because it was England but because of where we moved to. I had gone from living in an idyllic setting in the country to a housing estate in Southern England. Oh, joy! Not only transgender but Scottish too with accent, albeit with elocution lessons behind it and I already felt different in so many ways.

I found a real mix of kids at my new school. Everything was thrown into the melting pot here; nice kids, dodgy kids, scruffy kids, well dressed kids, intelligent, thick, caring, careless and the one downright nutter; the one who joined themselves onto me with highly sticky, invisible glue. That said, the school itself wasn't bad, just this one kid that no matter how hard I tried I could not shake off. There are always bullies and undesirable people but he was another breed altogether.

Why the huge jump in circumstances? It's not too long a story so I'll tell it. The local council put a compulsory purchase order on our land in Scotland which meant we had to sell it to them. They were planning to build a housing estate on it and we didn't want to be near it. This said, we didn't want to sell it to them straight away either as the Labour government were in and land prices were low.

Then along came (I say this tongue in cheek) good old Maggie Thatcher and land prices rocketed! By this time though, we were living in England with all our money tied up in land in Scotland. It was only after we had been down South for some time that we sold our land. After the money rolled in, my parents discussed the possibility of sending me back to private school. They decided against it as the next school I was to go to was so much nearer. They also didn't know what was going on with me either, and how could they if I didn't tell them?

By that time I was shot ten ways from knowing my backside from my elbow. My crazy 'friend' that latched on to me at primary school was still hanging around me like a nasty cold and was soon to become my unwanted buddy in so many ways I can't begin to tell you. I didn't stand a chance. Most of the kids hated him and tried to get me away from him. I tried but he just kept coming back like the damaged person he was. It felt easier to give into him than tell anyone because I was too ashamed of what was going on and afraid of fighting as well. Saying that, I did fight him a couple of times, told him to go away but 'no' was not an option. Not my choice of friend at all but no choice either. Everything was on his terms; friendship, sex, you name it.

My interest in girls started around the age of twelve. I have to admit that it was more because of the way they dressed and their hair that got me interested. I so wanted to dress up like them, to be like them but it was a fantasy that I rarely played out. My first girlfriend was at the age of fifteen. She was a year above me at school. I met her at the school disco and I asked her out. It was quite an experience for me and I discovered that I liked girls a lot more than boys, for many reasons. They seemed gentler, safer, not so likely to turn violent and abusive. I also felt more connected to them.

Confused I certainly was! I liked girls and wanted to be like them. This wasn't how it was supposed to be, I thought. I didn't want to grow up; it scared me rigid. I didn't want to be a man. I couldn't compete; men scared me. I found the men I knew to be unpredictable, unemotional creatures and the few that weren't, were usually gay which I didn't want to be like either. I hated wearing men's clothes and having their hairstyles and, at the same time felt compelled to mimic them. The end of school felt like the end of my life and my life was already miserable!

Magic & Mayhem

The move to England was a shock to my system as regards to having so much less space and freedom. There was still fun to be had though. I must admit I got more out of going on walks with Grandma than playing with my then, dodgy friends that I couldn't get shot of for love nor money.

The walks, as they were in Scotland, were quite magical. The countryside was different but full of unexplored territories. I came across abandoned buildings which I imagined contained treasure! My obsession with finding treasure has never diminished and I have gotten into trouble on many occasions for looking where I shouldn't.

Another love of mine was days out to the beautiful country houses, castles and ancient Roman villas around Sussex. When no one was looking, I'd be shoving at the wooden panelling in the old castles and houses to see if there was a secret passage behind. I never found one but I never stopped looking! There was another favourite haunt of mine which was an entire town built of reconstructed houses from different periods. Some were many centuries old. I loved the smell of the wood fires and to see the old implements that were used. I loved, and still love, old buildings; they have a soul, one can feel them.

I loved ghost stories too and my dad had many. His brother used to visit from Essex and when they got together they would talk about the old house in the Shetlands where they were born and of how haunted it was. *Windhouse*, now a ruin, is reported to have been one of Britain's most haunted houses. From the stories of things that had been seen, I am not surprised! A lot happened in that house a long time ago, and many of them were nasty things. It is now a sad, old neglected shell of a once grand place. I wanted to visit it but never got round to doing so. In the last ten or so years, the roof has gone and the harsh, Shetlandic winds have taken their toll. Because of the hauntings, I don't think anyone wanted to live in it and so it was abandoned, as far as I can make out.

The house we bought in Sussex had its fair share of hauntings too. I hated being alone in it for any length of time as there was a feeling of being watched. I was both intrigued and frightened by these goings on. The house wasn't that old but I feel that something must have happened on that piece of ground. My mum, dad and my grandma, who was a supreme sceptic when it came to ghosts, all had witnessed weird goings on there, such as footsteps coming up the stairs when no one else was around, strange pipe tobacco smells when no one smoked a pipe, disembodied laughter and talking. Anyway, enough about ghosts. We were near the sea too and I love water! I love getting wet, dodging the waves, skimming stones and generally playing with the sea. I had many exciting times, even with some of my dodgy mates, just playing by the sea.

The Big, Bad World!

I got a job as soon as I left school, working in a nursery that mostly grew tomatoes. I was sixteen years old. It was crap pay but undemanding in many ways, which I thought was great. 'This is what you do,' I thought, 'get a job, keep your head down, get drunk at every possible opportunity and that is your lot.' I was too intelligent for all that. I also had very few social skills and some fairly antisocial ones so, as quickly as I made friends, I made enemies. I was so bloody naïve and messed up!
I bounced out of that job after six weeks into another and another; all heavy manual labour that I wasn't suited for. I ended up on the YTS, a Youth Training Scheme; they were big in the eighties and took on every social dropout going. I fitted in and I liked it. I'll

never forget going for the interview though and walking into the main office. I was confronted by a couple of girls working in the office. They were about my age, one slightly older. I ached to be doing the job they were doing, to dress and look like they did, not signing up to do a painting and decorating course.

Some people ask me if I knew what was going on with me back then. How could I possibly? Do you remember the role models back then? Can you remember how gays, lesbians and transgender people were portrayed? No way, I wasn't like those freaks! The media always pick out the freaks. Normal people don't sell newspapers or create hyped up TV programmes for the arseholes and voyeurs of the world to watch.

No, I was well and truly in denial and lost. I had a best friend (other than the abusive one) who I was very attracted to but managed to mess that relationship up well and truly. I couldn't tell him how I felt about him or what was going on in my mind and I knew that one thing would lead to the other so I made an excuse to pick a blazing row with him and finished our friendship. He wouldn't have had anything to do with me anyway with the way I behaved sometimes. I gave out the type of antisocial behaviour that I had received; don't we all?

I bounced around for two years after leaving school, pretending to be fitting in and feeling like shit. I was drinking heavily and eventually my health broke. It was partly the drinking and mostly the stress of being someone in the wrong body for their gender. I broke out in eczema from head to foot. Bad eczema. I suffered like hell and was hospitalised for six months out of two years. One trip to hospital saw me in such a poor condition after a virus went systemic in my skin, that the doctor informed me I only had twenty-four hours to live, had I not been brought in. I spent four weeks and four days in an isolation room and another one week and three days in the ward.

Pain, you ask? Every time I woke up I cried because I didn't want to wake up. I just

wanted to die.

Hospital was a safe place for me; I didn't have to think about earning money in crap jobs, food was laid on and the dress code was pyjamas. Simple. I could opt out of life. It wasn't what I wanted but was the safest place I could live, I thought. It was undemanding, unchallenging, unlike the big and bigoted world of hateful, violent men, as I perceived them.

I was easy to bully; transgender women/girls generally are. We tend to be gentle souls from what I have experienced. Think of it this way; all people are on a gender spectrum so no one is completely male or female, they just can't be, it is not possible. There are myriad combinations in between, hence the reason we get some men or women that are quite masculine or feminine for their gender and others that are not. Transgender women tend to be, from what I can make out, really quite feminine in their mental make up although their biological bodies do not portray this. There are many men out there who are quite feminine, but not enough to make them feel they are in the wrong bodies. It has to be a considerable move to the opposite end of the spectrum to make someone wish to change their biological gender. These are my findings, it is not an absolute precis on the subject.

I digress. From there, hospital, I was discharged. Twenty years of age and terrified by the 'real world'; I use the term loosely. I always had a place in the St Thomas's hospital, London on the 11th floor. Leaving there filled me with dread. I was now under the care of the local hospital, which I have to say, turned out to be not too bad at all. It was a cottage hospital and the food etc was good. Another refuge but not what I wanted either. I was so ill when taken in, the other guys on the ward didn't think I'd make it. I was in a lot of pain and looked like shit; there was no other way to describe myself. That was aged twenty-eight and my last admission for acute skin disease.

Life (as I knew it).

When you're out there in your wellies
And feeling very camp,
And your barrow full of concrete
Just won't push up the ramp.

CHORUS:

You know you've got it wrong again
You know it just ain't right,
It's another path you've chosen
And it's covered in stinking shite!

Down the boozer and talking tough
There's a mean look in my eye.
I hope that no one cuts up rough
Oh, please, I'll surely die!

CHORUS

You know you've got it wrong again
You know it just ain't right,
It's another path you've chosen
And it's covered in stinking shite!

The Burton's suit fits so well
It's me, I am that man!
I'm Arthur, or Martha or the bloody Vandelas
Here we go again, oh damn!

CHORUS

You know you've got it wrong again
You know it just ain't right,
It's another path you've chosen
And it's covered in stinking shite!

The above is a little song I wrote to highlight the mistakes that I made when growing up. The awful jobs, the behaviours that didn't suit my personality and the female personality that didn't fit men's suits! Make of it what you will and please feel free to write or invent a tune as I don't have one for it.

On Being A Man

How does one be a man? I was taught that to be a man one had to do the following:

- Be able to drink plenty of beer, spirits etc.
- Shoot and kill animals.
- Talk abusively about women.
- Talk about sex in vulgar terms.
- Fight with men.
- Drive fast.
- Eat large portions of food.
- Act aggressively and swear a lot.
- Spit a lot.

- Do really menial jobs like working on building sites because it makes you look hard.
- Generally be a complete edjit; steal, lie and cheat where you can.

The above is so far removed from who I am as a person, I cannot even begin to tell you. I failed on nearly all levels apart from drinking heavily and eating large portions of food, just to try and fix the shitty way I felt about myself. The others I had a go at. Nothing I ever did regarding the above ever felt right or normal to me, and anyway, is that really the hallmark of a true man? Dear God, I hope not! From what I have seen, real men don't act this way; it is a bastardisation of how a man should be, a perversion to be more correct. No wonder I was lost.

Since discovering that real men don't actually act this way, it made me question if I could still 'be a man'. The answer came back to me as 'no, not possible, not the way I feel'. Many people have this expectation that if one is like me then that person will have a burning desire to have breasts and a vagina. More to the point, they view it as a requirement. 'Oh, yes', I have told people. 'I want big breasts and I'm so looking forward to having a vagina.' How the hell do I know if I want a pair of breasts and a vagina? I've never had them before for Christ-sake! People can be so stupid!

I started living my life as Katie and I changed my name on 14th October 2004. I started down the route of hormone therapy on 1st September 2006. I can only now tell you, in all heartfelt honesty, that a pair of breasts and a vagina sound like a good option! Either way it is irrelevant; my physical health is now too poor to contemplate such operations. When I started out on this journey though, and this is the bizarre and horrible thing of it, I was contemplating suicide if I could not go the whole way with all of the operations. Now that's not an option. What we do to fit in, eh? It's appalling.

Breast-wise, I already have a small pair due to hormone therapy and I am reasonably happy with them. I would like a little bigger pair but not overly so. The vagina I will just have to forget. It would be a huge mistake for me to attempt this kind of surgery with a damaged immune system and bad skin condition.

That's me then. Self improvement by self awareness and spirituality is where my challenge lies to do with my gender and sexuality; that's as far as it can go now on a physical level, at least as far as I can tell for the moment. Never say never! Who knows what the future holds and what I will be capable of changing later on.

Eczema - A living Hell

Mention eczema to many people and they picture a nasty little rash behind the knees, on the hands or at the elbow joints. Luckily, for many who suffer this affliction, that is all it is. For those like myself it is something far worse, and inhibits ones lifestyle to a great extent, and to the point of being disabling.

I have had severe eczema since I was two and a half years old. When I say severe, I am talking about all over my body. I am scarred for life in certain areas of my body due to trying to scratch the unbelievable and unrelenting itch. It leaves its scars mentally too.

In the past I have spent many months in hospital with the condition and have been put on cutting edge drugs and treatments that could have killed me. I am lucky to be alive and I don't say that lightly. I was lucky at school in the fact that I was never bullied because of it. A lot of kids had it then and in fact it was just accepted. I remember the first time that I dared to wear short trousers, much to my mum's horror and much thanks to an open minded teacher, some of the kids thought I had been badly burned. My legs were in a shocking state but again, it was just accepted. My mum was not so lucky at school and made to feel like a leper because of it and she only had it on her hands.

Well, here I am today and I still have the wretched thing. So many well meaning people come up with ideas about what might be causing it and how to cure it so I just smile, say 'thank you, I'll try that,' and move on. If you can think of it, I have probably tried it. A bit like people who try to help those with depression, I get the same thing. It is coming from a good place but is unhelpful and I'd rather that people just accepted what was going on with me.

Okay, I am an extreme case and some of what I have witnessed with it personally and with others in hospital is beyond belief. Also, the ignorance in the medical profession about how it affects people is pretty staggering. I have had doctors say to me, 'you need a job, that would sort this problem out,' when I looked and felt like I needed to be in hospital. I have been completely crippled with it in the past and had to beg for drugs. No one should have to face this type of mistreatment and humiliation.

No, severe eczema is severe eczema. It is severe when one is frightened to go to bed because removing one's clothes means removing skin from parts of the body or tearing at already broken flesh to try and cure an incurable itch. Not wanting to go out in public because one's face is swollen, red, raw and being frightened that I may make a scene because I can't stop myself from tearing at it. I have been literally suicidal with it at times in the past and that is no exaggeration. That is severe eczema.

Luckily, I am not that severe with it anymore on a regular basis but the times I am completely free from it are rare. It still affects my mental and emotional health, how could it not. It is very hard to be upbeat when one's face resembles a pizza and I get it on my face a lot!

I'm not a hundred percent sure why I wrote this but if it raises awareness of just how severe this condition can become and how people with severe eczema really suffer, then maybe that was why.

The Edge of The Wilderness

Between the ages of twenty and twenty-three were interesting times for me. Again, not particularly happy times, but better than what was to come.

At age twenty, I discovered Cornwall. I fell to her spell and eventually moved here. I came on holiday with my mum and grandmother. 'Grandma' had Alzheimer's disease and we were doing our lacking best to care for her one way or another. This was the only way we could all get a holiday. As was my want, I headed off down the pub of an evening and found a quite incredible drinking hole! It was full of interesting people that I felt were more accepting than the ones I had left 'up country'. They certainly weren't so up themselves. I remember the landlord asking me to come back at the new year as he would like to have dressed me up in a WRAF uniform. I got really excited at the thought of this; it sounded quite kinky! I never made it back for new year as my health was so ropey. I could commit to neither work nor pleasure and constantly lived off the State with bits of work thrown in when I could manage it. I thought about running off to Cornwall but knew in my heart that I was too unstable, both mentally and physically, to survive on my own. Living with my father and grandmother, with help from my mum, was far from ideal, but I was so codependent and emotionally needy that there was absolutely no chance of me living alone; I would have been a social services case in no time.

Twenty-one years old. What the fuck was that all about? I spent my twenty-first birthday in a social club with a friend, trying to get drunk, not feeling like it and wondering what the hell was to become of me now that I was a 'man'. Holy shit, I thought, what a ridiculous handle to stick on someone like me, and it was.

In an attempt to turn my life around, become a man, I took up training as a double glazing salesman. Another disaster! I went away for four days and nights to some country hotel near Manchester (no pun intended) where we were all supposed to be so grateful for being. I made a complete tit of myself. I had no idea how to act in this environment with these men and felt like a fish out of water. I was a nice person though, if more than a little eccentric and the guys made allowances for me and my rather odd behaviour, bless them!

In the field, in the big bad world of sales, I discovered that being a salesman was not all it was cracked up to be and found that more than a measure of dishonesty was required. One had to be able to con the shirt off a poor man's back and I couldn't bring myself to do it. I perceived this as yet another epic fail but in fact it wasn't. It told me more about the decent person I was trying so desperately to get away from, was so ashamed of.

By twenty-two, I was beginning to lose the plot. I now had little idea of who or what I was or how I expected to live my life. Between twenty-two and twenty-three was when my life changed dramatically. I awoke one morning and asked the question, 'What the fuck am I doing with my life? I am so unhappy. Nothing feels right to me. I can't even dress the way I want to. I am so not free. I don't even know if I am straight or gay or even if I am allowed to ask that question.' That last bit made me fucking angry. Why should anyone not be allowed to ask any question? To cut to the chase as they say, or get to the meat of it, that was when I lost the plot on an ever increasing scale. What caused my rapid decline into insanity and some of the most bizarre behaviour, was shame. People with unhealthy amounts of shame do the most fucked up things (is there a HEALTHY amount?). Shame is responsible for most of society's violence and addiction; that I firmly believe. People who do not live in shame live in freedom. Society and the media have become more shaming as time goes on. 'My God, is that all you can afford?' says the media and everyone goes into shame and goes out to buy more of the shit that is being advertised. 'How male are you? How female are you? How fat, how tall, how small?' says the shouty box in the corner that controls and sedates the masses on a daily basis. 'Buy all this shit, look like this/him/her and you will be happy.' What a fucking bare-faced lie! The only people getting happy, are the ones coining it in from the poor mugs eager to feel better about themselves that were absolutely fine to start with, before the media got to their fragile egos. As I see them, the large businesses and corporations that dominate the world are nothing more than parasites living off people's misery.

My Descent Into Madness

Twenty-three years old and my life had plumbed even more miserable depths. I was now heading for a psychotic breakdown. I told a lot of my drinking buddies and
anyone else who would listen, that I was gay. It was one of the most uncomfortable things I have ever done because it wasn't true. So, why do it? I naïvely thought that if people thought I was gay they wouldn't bother if I started wearing women's clothes etc. Naïve doesn't even go there, does it? Bigots are bigots.

It was a pointless thing to do anyway as I only ever went out dressed as a woman to a gay pub a few miles away where I felt safe. I became increasingly paranoid as to what people thought of me for 'being gay'.

As I write this and look back I can hardly believe what was going on with me. I was riddled with shame but could not recognise it for what it was. I was too ashamed of being ashamed of myself to be able to see it. I thought I had to be gay if I wanted to dress as a woman. I constantly analysed myself to see what I felt and 'how feminine I was'. I was going nuts at a fast rate of knots. I spoke to anyone and everyone that would listen about my confusion and plight. Note 'confusion'; this was something I would never admit to as I was brought up to feel that it was shameful not to know what was going on for me. Why didn't I know how I felt and what I wanted?

So the descent into madness continued. Many friends were patient with me, with my bizarre behaviour and talk. Some people just ridiculed me behind my back. Others, who pretended to be friends but in fact had issues of their own, tried to tell me that I was imagining stuff that wasn't there and of course I was straight. One of these pretend friends started to open up one night about his own experiences and then very quickly shut down again. All began to come clear; he had no interest in where I was coming from at all and was more concerned that if someone who looked like me could be gay, bisexual or transgender or wherever I was at that point, could he be too?

One of my friends figured this guy out to be a shit and he was correct. You're not going to believe this but do you know I slept with quite a few gay men for no other reason than that is what I thought I should be doing? It's beyond fucked up I know, but it is true. I was lucky not to catch something nasty although I was pretty careful.

There were also a few occasions where I was lucky not to have gotten attacked or arrested, take your pick. My behaviour was very random as I was binge drinking and abusing prescribed drugs. I smoked a bit of weed from time to time but it had the nasty side effect of making me even more paranoid than I already was. By age twenty-four, I was so mentally ill that I thought I was shouting stuff out in the street when I wasn't. I would walk along with my fingers in my mouth to stop myself shouting things even though I was told by friends that I wasn't. Again it was all shaming stuff. I thought I was shouting things like 'I'm gay' or 'queer' or even nasty things about myself that weren't true, again always to do with an accent on sexual conduct.

I was LMFAO, Lost, Mental, Fucked-up And Out-there! What I went through I would not wish upon anyone.

Out of The Wilderness

At age twenty-seven, I had a huge change in lifestyle. I hit the wall, so to speak, and realised that life wasn't working out. I had dispensed with long hair and decided to give up drinking. So, I started to live my life as a 'man' and joined AA to give up the booze. Both things were necessary at that time to help me move on one way or another, but I was in a tremendous amount of mental anguish as I was not being true to myself in any way shape or form. I gave up the booze (the symptom) and contained all the shame and confusion inside (the root cause of my dis-ease).

Shortly after joining AA I met a girl who was two years older than me and only two weeks more sober and I asked her out. We started dating and all went well for the first couple of weeks. To be absolutely honest, if I hadn't met her I would not have stayed around the fellowship, as at that time I felt I had nothing to live for. In a way it was true; there is only one life to live and if we are not being true to ourselves and being ourselves, what is the point?

A couple of weeks into the relationship we went for a drink, a soft drink, in a 'safe' pub where everyone knew she wasn't drinking and where she was staying in between moving home. The evening was going well until she suddenly looked behind me and said, 'Oh, look! I just have to introduce you to my friends at that table over there. One of them is my best mate.'

I looked behind me and went stone cold. I knew them too and they only knew me as 'Jennifer' from the gay bar in town! She grabbed me by the hand and pulled me over to introduce me. I wanted the floor to open up and swallow me.

It's a long story but the upshot of it all is that her 'best mate' told her all after she pumped him for information the next day. My biggest fear, which I had pretty much resigned myself to being a reality, did not happen; she didn't dump me! Our relationship was short lived though and not because of that. Neither of us were in a place to hold down any kind of commitment that way; we were both too screwed up, but we did remain friends.

Still Crazy But Safe

The four and a half years I spent in AA, from 1995 – 2000, were some of the better years of my early adult life but by no means happy. I was ill at ease with myself and desperate to explore myself, but my feelings were so shut down and I was entrenched in a shame cycle. I started doing the old thing of sharing in meetings that I was gay for no other reason than I thought I should be gay and therefore people would understand why I wanted to dress in women's clothes. Of course, it made me exceedingly uncomfortable because it wasn't true. I was just as uncomfortable with sharing that I was transgender, which became another well told story of mine, not because it wasn't true but I didn't have the emotional connection and tools to really understand how I felt, or who I was, at anything other than a peripheral depth, and even that was a struggle!

All said and done, I was totally obsessed with my story and self analysis. Again, like my old drinking days, I would talk to anyone and everyone who would listen. I was emotionally and mentally quite unwell and suffered extreme anxiety and panic attacks. I was still in the awful place of thinking I was shouting things out in the street. I would love to have gotten real help but I thought if I told a professional the exact state of my mental health I would be given dangerous drugs or, worse, put in a place where I was made to take dangerous drugs with dire side effects; creating yet another problem instead of solving the initial one. In hindsight, I think I was right to keep my mouth shut; I've seen the bad side effects of psychoactive drugs to 'help people' and it's not pretty. I'm not saying they are not beneficial for some because they are, but it's not my bag. I had a very bad trip on an antidepressant drug back then which turned me manic and I will never forget it. Big Pharma, you can shove your psychoactive drugs where the sun doesn't shine!

Although AA gave me a safe place to be for those years, I didn't like it. I got a lot of help from some good people, some bad experiences from some not so nice people, but all in all a better life than I had been leading. Still absolutely no self esteem to write home about and my physical health was, as it still is, not very good either.

I made a very good, honest friend in AA, someone who trusted me unconditionally and with whom I hung out on a regular basis. She wasn't full of the false recovery that some of the people were and was honest about how she felt. Spiritual programmes are great but as I have found out to my cost at times, fools with large egos and a little knowledge can be very dangerous people indeed, especially if one is vulnerable. A spiritual programme is every bit as effective at keeping people entrenched in their own madness as it is for getting them free from it, if it is used wrongly. There are a few deluded people in twelve step programmes who have not taken drink or drugs for a very long time but are convinced that anyone with less time than they have around the scene has absolutely nothing to tell or teach them. Wrong! We all have a message to carry and wisdom to impart. The Twelve-Step Fool is easy to spot; they have their fingers in their ears and their mouths wide open. There is nothing to say to them because they cannot hear you. This aside, if in need and if one can find a good sponsor, a twelve-step programme can turn one's life around; it certainly did mine and for that I am truly grateful. In no way do I mean to lessen the positive impact that twelve-step programmes have on the lives of many. Miracles happen in these gatherings; I have witnessed it and been a part of it. I digress. My dear friend Emma took me under her wing and heard my story, shared hers with me and we had some fantastic days together. I used to look after her house when she went away on holiday. It was a great privilege as she was trusting me with some reasonably valuable antiques. I had the run of the house and it was in a beautiful location but I was alone and without anything to take the edge off my feelings. When one is emotionally and mentally as screwed as I was, I don't recommend sitting alone with your feelings. When the paranoia creeps in and the shadows are moving, your head is spinning and the fear and anxiety are tearing your mind apart, alone is not a good place to be.

Sometimes I would sit in a chair and rock back and forth with my poor, fucked head in my hands. I slept a lot back then. I quite often had to have an afternoon nap and still do some days.

Emma encouraged me to write and to paint. This was something that was a saviour to me; gave me a purpose and a place to stand in the world. I saw myself for what I was for the first time in many years; a writer and an artist! That was who I was (part of me anyway). I started to dress like an artist and become a bit more flamboyant, even though I was still very uncomfortable with myself but I felt more real. I took great inspiration from a designer by the name of Lawrence Llewellyn Bowen. I thought this man was just fabulous. He looked great, sounded great and had taste to die for! Yep, I had found my temporary role model...

Finding My Wings – Meeting Susan

It was one of the best things I did, meeting Susan. I was at a stage in my life where I was crying out for independence but dying of codependence! It wasn't a match made in heaven and she didn't really know what she was taking on, although I did tell her about me and my issues with having a growing need to cross-dress. I had to tell her because we were planning to live together. It is not wise to even try to repress such an urge nor is it healthy, and I knew that if this part of me was going to have to hide in this relationship then we would fall apart quickly. As it was, she never really did accept me for who I was and in all honesty, she needed a man and that was something that I just played at being.

There was a lot of love between us and, indeed, we are still friends although we see little of each other now. That relationship, along with our move to Cornwall, probably saved my life. I had to grow up and fast! Even though I still suffered from acute anxiety attacks, skin problems and chronic fatigue, I had to get myself together and get work. There was also the business of the house that Susan bought; it needed quite a lot of work doing to it and yours truly was experienced in the building trade.

Yes, it all happened at once. Three months after moving to Cornwall, I had landed myself a job as a part time housekeeper with a lovely family and had a house to do up. Take into account that I had never lived away from home for any length of time, apart from a bedsit near Bognor Regis which turned out to be an epic fail after three months. I had also never held down a relationship for longer than three months.

The same was pretty much true of my working career; I was just not capable of holding down anything, either from a physical or mental health point of view.

Cornwall is not an easy place to live. So many people idealise it, and it is idyllic but it has an energy that demands change of anyone who comes here. Change is what we both got, in so many areas of our lives. It was all a big gamble but it paid off. I ended up with a life which I would not otherwise have had and Susan ended up with a property that sold for at least two and a half times what she paid for it and no mortgage. In that sense we were both winners but the relationship was on rocky ground from not too long after we moved. In reality, how could it have been anything else?

Leaving Susan

Leaving Susan was one of the hardest decisions I have made in life. Not because I thought there was a chance of the relationship working but because I had never lived on my own before for any considerable length of time. That time was short, a one-off experience and within easy reach of home. I had little or no budgeting skills either. I knew what to buy to make a home and I did a good job economically.

Leaving was scary but I had a bit of luck to start with that sort of eased me into it. I needed to get out and a friend of ours said that her boyfriend had a spare room he could offer me while I was looking around. I feared I wouldn't get the room as he found out that I was cross-dressing and became worried about what I might be wearing at his place. I was frightened of being homeless and he was frightened about what I was going to wear – compared to me, he had a very high class problem!

Saying that, he turned out to be a real saviour; good company and a down to earth Cornishman. The time I spent there gave me a little well-needed time to get my head together.

So, I spent the first seven weeks of self-reliance in Newlyn. I still had my job as a housekeeper and was still involved with the village hall where I used to live but needed to find a place of my own. I have seen places I would not house an animal in that people are expected to pay high rents for; it is disgusting and so are some of the people who rent them out. I turned down one sizeable bedsit through hesitation and kicked myself for it afterwards, wondering if I would ever find another like it. Again, in hindsight, I'm glad I did turn it down as it wasn't in the best location and something far better came up.

The place I got was a bedsit but it was the king of bedsits. This was a luxury pad indeed! I had a landlady who was very caring. She also had more crazy schemes than one could shake a stick at and dragged me into one or two of them. It did me a lot of good as it kept me from going too much into myself.

You know, it's really sad looking back at this time, as it makes me aware of the prejudice there was at that time. Things still aren't brilliant but they are better. It was only in 1998 that the human rights bill came into being and people like me could no longer be thrown out of their homes and jobs and generally, but legally, receive abuse because they were transgender. This was 2004. I remember feeling the need to explain to her that I was now going to live my life as Kate (my current name, Katie, came later as I felt it was too girly for me at that time). I also remember thinking that I may not be allowed to do this under the same roof as her and her husband and I might just have to move out, human rights or not. Another nail biting, fucked up scary time! As it happened, they were both very understanding people who generally sided with the underdog. So, life went on.

Lies & Doctors

I was not honest with my doctor or anyone else when I started down the road of hormone treatment. In fact, long before this, when I was dipping a metaphorical toe in the water in my mid twenties, I can remember telling a whole pile of steaming bullshit to a female counsellor about how much I masturbated about being a woman! This is embarrassing stuff to look back on. I then worried that it would look like I was kinky and I thought (wrongly) that transgender people were not meant to have kinks. So, back I went for another go and told them that I had lied about masturbating about it and came out with another load of bullshit.

The bottom line is, I was terrified. I had visions of being forced into some kind of role without being able to find my way or be allowed to explore myself. I feared that the doctors, shrinks and whoever else might be involved would make me 'do stuff I wasn't comfortable with'. After all, it was the story of my life; every son of a bitch I seemed to run into had something crap lined up for me. I was vulnerable, knew it but couldn't admit it, and was not prepared to let anyone else 'have a go' at me with their shitty ideas about how I should be. Again, the story of my life. So I went back into my crazy, messed up shell.

When I finally got round to doing something about changing sex, I approached it with all the same fears and very little more self knowledge about what I wanted. I had transgender friends who kept me right. This was lucky because most of the local doctors et al knew bugger all and, as stated earlier, I was sent to a man, an endocrinologist, who in hindsight, didn't really have a foggy clue what he was tackling. Bless him, he used to get me in, do all the appropriate bloods etc but then he used to look at my hairline to see if it had advanced forward or not. He even got me to take my top off to see if my breasts were growing! Jaw dropping stuff when I look back. Thank God I had those friends who kept me right and got me to search further afield for proper clinics. Without them, and this is no word of a lie, I would have been dead; I don't think I could have gone through it all without them. You know what, I even lied to them through fear sometimes because I just wanted to fit in. Sad, huh?

I have found out that I am not alone in this and that many, if not everyone who has been on this journey that I know about or have heard of, have told some whopping fibs! Such is the fear that they will be manipulated into something they don't want to do or are not ready for. The confusion; another thing strongly denied by many, is quite profound. Why would it not be? We are not brought up to recognise such things in ourselves and we have little or no true peers or role models, save for the media-hyped eccentrics that make a great story but are of very little other use to the transgender cause. We think that we should have outright knowledge of who we are and exactly where we want to go in life regarding our gender. Why on earth should we? Many I know have gotten to a ripe old age and not even discovered what they want as a career or found the right partner to meet their needs or even really know who they are as a person. These things unfold as we go along in life, that is, if we are allowed the time and space to discover them without being bullied into making false decisions.

Kinks

Have you ever wondered what a kink is or where they come from? Have you ever pondered the morality or ethics of them? Do you view them as bad, good, healing or harming? So many thoughts and judgements are made on them.

I believe that kinks come from 'things that we are not meant to be doing but in some way give us pleasure'. They are naturally occurring. Religion has tried to shame us out of them over the years with the idea of 'sin'. Unfortunately for the religion, it doesn't cure these kinks, it only adds shame and guilt to the person who has them. It can also suppress the kink, which creates in the person an unhealthy dislike of that aspect of themselves. Yes, it comes back to negativity breeding negativity.

I have a kink that started way back as long as I can remember. I do not know how it started, only that it did. It is as about as harmless as one can get unless, as I did, one becomes ashamed of it. Sex is one of the most natural acts that one can think of. Sex without intercourse is where the trouble seems to lie. We judge ourselves so harshly if sexual pleasure is taken from anything other than the missionary position. After all, it is just an emotion and a pleasure.

I used to experience a certain pleasure from dressing up, even as a young child. I cannot say it was sexual as I did not have sexual desires at the age of four but I did experience something quite profound. The pleasure from wearing certain materials and clothing that I got was unmistakeable. Also, the smells that the material itself had, used to make me want to wear them. Most people do not talk of such things but I do not know why as they are perfectly harmless. Maybe it could be our old enemy 'shame'? After all, self-pleasuring of any sort is looked on as unacceptable. Let us not forget that those sort of pleasures are also, consciously or unconsciously, associated with the Feminine! Yes, that old demon has reared its head, threatening the masculine yet again. How dare it!

I wish to take you a little deeper now, into the world of energies and energetic forces. This is where I am going with my thread. When I was dressing up, I felt connected to something wonderful and joyful. No, not Satan. Pleasure is not evil or the work of the Devil! I actually feel the need to explain this as so many people are indoctrinated against pleasure. I digress. What I felt was 'connected'. It was like a part of me was missing, and when I was dressing up, I was then whole, complete. In hindsight, always the best as they say, I believe that I was connecting to my root chakra. The root chakra is linked with sexual energy, Earth energy and vitality. People have been wrongly taught and shamed into thinking that sexual energy is all about having sex, pretty much the way that they have been taught that anger is wrong because it means violence and destruction when in fact, if used properly, it is a source for the recognition of wrong-doing and change. Anger can also be used, if channelled correctly, for creativity. Sexual energy is no different. It can be highly productive, excuse the pun.

Sexual energy is manifested in so many ways; the way people choose to dress, art, speech and even bodily posture. We even build homes and offices that reflect our earthly connection (mind you, I don't know what that says about your average building developer). The rooms of our homes are vibrant, or not, with our root chakra connection. This energy is inescapable but can be denied and blocked. I know and have known people with a blocked root chakra, whose connection to Earthly energies are but little and it does not do them any favours. I have also experienced this myself. That said, there is a balance needed. All of the other energies are needed too. No one can survive on bread alone so connect with the universe; there is so much wonder out there!

Have It Their Way

Judged and guilty of fornication
You've been condemned to hell's damnation,
Caught in bondage, tied in rope
Heaven's gates are beyond hope.

Don't risk being shunned for being gay
Just shut yourself down, watch what you say,
Don't wear whatever turns you on
Fear the thugs and religion's con.

Don't walk the path you feel you should
Swap good for bad and bad for good,
Stand on high ground, judge the others
Forget they are your sisters and brothers.

Sexy thrills are just depraved
Don't be yourself, it's ill behaved,
Always fear what others may say
And lurk in the sump of Sanity Bay.

Have It YOUR Way!

Why not have a thrill a day,
Be sexy, daring or downright gay?
Oh, to live life free from fetter
But sometimes handcuffs can be better!

Fear not the judgement and disdain
Of those who'd wish us hate and pain.
Hearts, fly free and swift as a dove
The God I understand is love!

So what's the harm in a bit of bondage?
A slight rope burn might need a bandage.
A bit of play with a teacher's cane
Hardly writes one off as insane.

Get hit with pies and covered in soup
Followed by custard and spaghetti hoop,
Life is more than just to survive
Make others smile 'cause you feel alive!

The erotic love of being gay
The sacred beauty of same sex play,
To wear the clothes that turn us on
Go, live YOUR life, be glad you're born!

Dirty Drugs & Incompetence

The three plus years of hell I went through on synthetic oestrogen was indescribable! Sheer abject hell is close though. I was prescribed Ethinylestradiol by an endocrinologist in Truro, Cornwall. I should have been sent to Exeter gender clinic right at the start but no one had any information on it, including my endocrinologist. It was a transgender friend, who possibly saved my life come to think of it, that made me aware of them. A straightforward shift across you think? Oh, no! I then had to battle the NHS through my Local MP to get an appointment.

I digress. Back to those horrendous drugs. If you have ever suffered SJS; Steven Johns Syndrome, you will know of the horrors I went through. Not once but about a dozen times. I melted an ice pack from the freezer in five minutes in front of a friend one night. I felt like my whole body was on fire. It is the most horrific thing to see the rapid changes that take place with it:

- I started clawing at the skin on my face and neck until it was raw, weeping and bleeding.
- Incredibly fast facial swelling.
- Temperature rapidly rising to an unbearable point.
- Skin sloughing off my whole body and still going mad with the itch and clawing at it.

I was lucky enough to be living with my mum while all this was going on, otherwise I would have been severely screwed. Someone asked me if I ever took any pictures or got someone to take pictures of me in this condition. You have to be joking! No way was I letting anyone near me with a camera in this condition. These bouts lasted up to two weeks in some cases; the severe swelling going down after about a week. The mood swings I had with it were incredible too but that could have been because I was so traumatised by it. Never have I suffered, or want to suffer again anything like it. Believe it or not, I managed to hold down two part-time jobs with all this shit going on. One was a cleaning job for a very understanding agency. The other was a delivery job for a large corporation who didn't give a shit about what was going on with me, told me so and made a suggestion for me to get a friend to do my round for me while I was ill. That was highly against their so-called policy, and all the crap would have hit me should it have gone wrong, but it didn't and here I am. The delivery job is long gone. Good riddance!

Unhealthy Expectations

There is a crazy requirement, or at least expectation, that gender clinics and the government have of transgender people. That is, to be in employment, or at least seeking it, early on in the journey. When I first came out, I was already in employment. That didn't last long and was nothing to do with my gender reassignment journey. The people I worked for fell into cash flow problems due to unforeseen circumstances and I was made redundant. I hate having nothing to do and quickly got some cleaning jobs etc. My health was failing again at that point and I soon had to give them up.

After a short stint on the sick, I signed on. The pressure on me to get a job was quite unbearable though and I was forced into voluntary work with a view to this increasing my chances of employment. My mental and emotional health was not all it could have been by a long shot and I found it hard to cope, even with voluntary work. The government never take into consideration the emotional stress one is under when changing sex or the prejudice one is likely to encounter when job seeking, nor do they really care. I think it is their perverse idea of 'equality'. When changing sex, many of us are not equal to the average person in the street and we struggle. The fittest survive and the weakest sink. It is grossly unfair to expect someone to go out into the workplace at the beginning of their gender reassignment journey. Voluntary work in a suitable environment by all means, but not paid work unless again, that person really feels they can handle it. A lot of transgender people are fighters; we've bloody had to be to survive and will not admit to feeling vulnerable. We will have a go anyway. One of my placements in the voluntary field was great. It was among really understanding people and I worked in an office raising money for their charity. I had a fab person to work beside and we raised a lot of cash and had a good time.

I was put on another placement, working with the homeless and disadvantaged people in Camborne and that too was very rewarding but I was not mentally ready for it and suffered as a result. I should never have been allowed to go near the place. Myself and a lot of the workers there were consuming about as much alcohol as some of the homeless people we were trying to help! It was chaos on all sides some days. I was totally wracked with anxiety and stressed beyond belief. My head spun and I found it difficult to drive home at the end of shifts (not because of the alcohol I might add; I used to save that until the evening).

I remember leaving that position. It came to the point where I had to admit to myself that I couldn't cope. My self esteem was rock bottom and I can remember thinking that I wouldn't be missed. I was wrong. A couple of the clients there were really choked. One nearly cried and said how much she would miss seeing me. I felt awful but knew that I was doing the right thing. It was a huge learning curve and one I don't regret in any way.

Where I Am Now

Friday 14th March 2014.

So, where am I at now? My physical health is still ropey and I still struggle with anxiety and bouts of depression but I feel I am coping better with life than I have done for a while.

What really gets me down is the eczema on my face. If I may say so myself, I have quite an attractive face with quite feminine features but when my face is swollen, like it is now, I lose the feminine features and I see the old me again. This is hard to take, I don't like it at all. This really messes with my state of mind and I hate going out when I'm like this. It kicks off all my old paranoia and self-esteem issues. The fear of negative comments puts me on edge.

What would I like to see for the future? I would like to see transgender people feeling more able to be open and honest with themselves and their doctors without the fear that decisions will be made for them, treatment rejected and their lives snatched from their hands. Also, doctors knowing where to refer transgender people and not making assumptions about them or trying to tackle their issues when they don't have a clue how to treat them.

I'd like better emotional, relationship and sexual education in schools. Not the outdated stuff they have been regurgitating for eons. Wider understanding that LGBTQs (Lesbian, Gay, Bisexual, Trans and Questioning) are not made, they are born this way.

The other thing we have to contend with is the media; the images that are flashed at us constantly of how we should be and look. Now, here's a thing. Most of us are caught in the trap of how we look. The one thing I have tried to do is achieve a regular look. What I mean is reaching a place where having a face full of sores is more of an anomaly than a regularity so that my facial shape does not change so much and so often. Day to day, how I look is a bloody lottery and I'm gut sick of it. I feel like I lose my femininity again and again. I'm transgender for God's sake, I don't have a lot to work with from the word go without all this.

I write this on Saturday 15th March 2014. All in all, today has been a good day. I live in a beautiful house, have eaten healthily and played down the beach with my friend. Take that into account and things look brighter. Here's to better times! Here's to a more understanding world in which to live!

Monday 17th March – I'm not going to start a diary here, just give a snapshot of how life is for me at the moment. I am again on the mend from facial eczema and the relief is great. I am looking forward once more. Sometimes staying in the moment is crap if one is suffering in that moment. It is easy to forget that I have, when things are going well, a lot of people in my life and much going on if I should wish to get out there and get into it. Today, I shall rest, eat a pasty and do things that please me. I also have the love of my little cat, Izzy.

I am loved, I must remember this in down times. I am a competent administrator where I work, I am a writer by trade, a Reiki healer and so much more. If I had not taken the decision to be myself, I would have held much back from the world. If we are not allowing ourselves to be who we are, that is exactly what is happening; we are not giving to the world the gifts that we have been given by God to share with His or Her creations.

I also must remember that to have consciousness is the greatest gift. It can never be taken from us when we have it. This is the life source. This is why I can be grateful, whether I am in emotional or physical pain. Now and then, I forget this. So, I am now grateful. What a gift! This is worth rejoicing about!

I suppose I should also tell you, the reader, what has happened to me over the last few years, just to sum up. Quite a lot actually. I haven't sat twiddling my thumbs. I want to take us back to May 27th 2002. That was the day I moved to Cornwall. This was a pivotal point in my life and the move that really saved my life. I discovered that I could cope in so many ways that I had not guessed possible. Sometimes it takes letting go, taking a chance and doing something scary to make a change. All things come to pass.

I also want to take us back to around 2009. I had been back on a twelve-step programme for about four years by then and I was starting to struggle. Not with any kind of abstinence but with life in general. I needed to move forward; not with a career but with my view of life. I was 'stuck'. I know people bang on about having a sponsor in these fellowships but it really is a good idea if one wants to progress. I'd had a couple of sponsors and had outgrown them. Their ways were okay. But it was their ways and I needed someone to teach me how to discover 'my ways'. That I found in one of the most incredible women I have ever encountered. She knew how to work a spiritual programme without getting into her ego and her stuff. That, my friends, is a rare species of human being. In the end she let me go but it was nothing that I had done wrong; she had merely taken on too many sponsees. What she taught me in the time that I was with her, changed the way that I view the world, even to this day. I would like to say a huge thank you to her as she not only changed my life but probably saved it too.

The end of 2009 saw me move out of my mother's home, where I had stayed for three years, and move to the centre of Penzance. This move was colossal for me. I had never really lived on my own for any appreciable length of time before without alcohol or cigarettes to prop me up or a relationship holding it together, so imagine what a step it was for me. I'll never forget that lovely little, incredibly haunted flat either, and the times I had there. I loved it, it was special to me and I have fond memories of it. Bless my lovely neighbours too. I grew in that place.

1st November 2010 saw me get a contract with my current employers. I have been with the same organisation working part-time for over four years now! Can you even begin to understand what that means to me? Bloody hell, I held down a job THAT long! A few days after that, I met a very pretty woman who became my girlfriend. It was one of the most nail biting roller-coaster rides I have had but I do not regret it. It lasted for nearly two years with two break ups and so much crazy shit at the end that I do not know where to start. I do not see her any more and have no desire to. We are best left to live separate lives.

Now, I live in a wonderful, beautiful home with a loyal, insightful friend who has encouraged me to write my life story. I have the most amazing and loving cat, Izzy, whom I love to bits. My relationship with my mum is still great and I value her so much for just being there. I still live in Penzance, by the way. I love

Cornwall, and like most of the people that live here I cannot abide the greedy developers and bankers that want to destroy our pleasant land. Cornwall is not for everyone so please stay away if you only think of it as a quaint place for a second home or somewhere to make cash out of. Cornwall is a way of life as well as a place that will teach you its ways so, if you move here and cannot adapt to it, it will chew you up and spit you out.

Well, that's all folks! God and good fortune willing, there might even be another book in the offing, who knows? Thank you for reading and I hope you got much from my work and my life.

Part Two

Flowers

Life In General

The first few pages are a little harrowing, I get that, but that was how life was. I'm not saying there weren't any good times but most of my life was spent being someone else and living in fear of being discovered. It is an unimaginable way to live. I was trapped in the wrong body for my gender and unable to express myself. If you want to make someone mentally and physically ill, stop them expressing themselves; that'll do the job nicely!

Yep, sexual relationships happened but were unfulfilling in many ways. Let's face it, how could it be anything else if your sexual organs do not match your sexual needs? I loved and still love women but sex with them just used to leave me feeling very confused. Society taught me that sex with the same sex was wrong and I felt a great affinity with women; very connected to them. I couldn't explain it but I felt that what I was doing was wrong. Having sex with women wasn't wrong but the indoctrination had got through, even at that subconscious level. Also, I felt that penetrative sex was not what I should be doing and didn't know why; it never felt right. Saying that, I have since become very okay with it for two reasons: 1) It would not be a wise idea for me to go through the sex change operation. 2) I see it as an expression of love so what is 'wrong' with expressing love? (This question is rhetorical. If you do have a problem with what I have just said I do not wish to hear the filthy outpourings of your troubled mind so keep it to yourself)!

Sex with men, well that came later but to tell the truth there were many times that I was so switched off that I could have been having sex with a chair. Yes, some of it was really hot, male or female but I never ever felt like I was being me or that the other person was really getting me.

My one regret? I met a gorgeous looking guy in hospital when I was twenty. We were having coffee one day in the cafeteria. I suspected he had a thing for me because of the way he looked at me and touched me sometimes. That afternoon over coffee he told me that he would like to make love to every part of my body. I was red hot with excitement. I looked him in the eyes, told him I was straight and that it wasn't my thing but I didn't mind him fancying me. What utter bullshit! I was terrified of being caught, that was all. What a shit way to live.

On the plus side, I met a beautiful blonde women in the same hospital who was ten years older than me and we had quite a thing going on in there! If I talk a lot about the hospital I apologise but it was the best times I had back then, sad as that may sound; I could hide there. On the outside, I did jobs that didn't suit me and drank myself to oblivion at every opportunity as I thought that was how a man should behave and anyway, it was a way to escape life.

I never wanted to grow up. I loved being a child but again I wasn't happy because I could never really express who I was by dressing the way I wanted. I needed to explore my gender even as a child. What the fuck is so amazing about that? Doesn't everyone? Yes, they do but my type of exploration wasn't acceptable.

Do I sound angry? No shit! Well done Sherlock for picking up on that. No one should have to live this way and yet so many are forced to because of society's bigotry. It isn't just the straights that give out prejudice towards transgender people, it's also some of the lesbians and gays too. Bisexuals are more understanding because they get shit from the lesbian and gay scene as well. You would think that they would naturally understand what was going on but no; for some reason there are many of them who feel threatened by us. Although I have had many lesbian friends over the years, some lesbians I have found to be the worst when it comes to bigotry. It's so ironic when some of them won't accept me as a women and yet some of them are so like men (but you can't say that, it wouldn't be politically correct). The same goes for some of the gay guys I've encountered who do not accept me as female, it's fucking pathetic. They just can't get over their own issues because in some way I don't think they have really accepted who they are or know very much about themselves. A lot of this is down to piss-poor sex education in schools and again, this is down to bigotry and control by those with the power to do differently. While we are at each other's throats, we are pliable and up for manipulation. 'Look what the queers are doing to us!' What exactly? Bringing you shows and entertainment (they've got natural art you know), literature, paintings, working in your shops, hospitals and factories, fighting your shitty wars and generally adding to the economy. Is that what the gay and trans communities are doing to you? Is that what the queers are up to?

Open your eyes, you've been blinded!

Victims

One of the things I've been reminded of on my journey is 'victims'. Whenever someone has been victimised, like I have, the victim can also 'about-face' and become a perpetrator, such as I did. My life is by no means blameless and I have hurt a lot of people on my way. Even at school, when I was bullied because I didn't fit in, I found dubious release in bullying others. My life was made a misery and I helped to make a misery of others lives too. Bullying is a disease that perpetuates itself on a false feeling of power. I get bullied so I feel powerless. Not having the tools to be able to deal with it I go on to bully others.

It was a constant theme at school for me, bullying. School was abusive. I was caught in a trap of having little to no support and too frightened to say what was going on or how I felt so I re-enacted what was going on. I can remember on many occasions calling another child a poof, a fucking queer etc etc. Horrible I know and it may be difficult for you, the reader, to comprehend why I did it when I clearly had gender/sexuality issues myself.

The simple answer is that I was covering up and trying to hide what I was and how I felt in a grim and desperate attempt to offset what was happening. I was terribly vulnerable and in desperate need of understanding and support, not to mention protection, but I hurt some others too.

My casualties I ran into after I left school, in various circumstances, and I didn't like what I had done. I could see the hurt, pain and anger in their faces and it made me feel ashamed. These people that I had hurt were like me, not necessarily anything other than straight but gentle beings who only wanted to help people. That still haunts me sometimes and I guess it should. If there is such a thing as healthy shame, then that is what I feel regarding my behaviour. Self-forgiveness is the toughest thing to achieve and I am still working on it. I keep reminding myself that I did the best I could with what I had to work with and I believe I did, though I have to keep reminding myself.

One particular 'victim' of mine went on to become a St John ambulance volunteer. That was the last I heard of him. He was just the type, a decent person. I met him on the bus one day and saw the look he gave me. There are no words to describe how I felt. I so wanted to say sorry for being such an arsehole but I could see by the look in his eyes that words would never be enough to heal the deep emotional wounds I had caused. That look still haunts me and I would do virtually anything to put that situation right. That was at least twenty years ago. Be sure your past will catch you up!

For one to hurt another so badly, one has to be hurting that badly, or worse, oneself. It is not a natural act to violate someone so deeply. I had been violated, there is no question of that, and that is how I was so capable of inflicting pain. When we are traumatised at such a deep level, our emotional reasoning may not always be completely compromised, but our ability to decipher what is appropriate or

right and wrong at an intellectual level can, and mine was. We can
go against what we feel to do something that is ultimately wrong
because we think we should be doing it. This may seem like a
paradox and I grant you it is. Only sad experience can avail you of
this terrible enlightenment.

A Hidden Blessing

I mentioned having a friend that I couldn't get rid of a while ago. I
am never certain whether he was a blessing or a curse. In many
ways I feel that he was both. Without him in my life I guess I could
have gone either way: found my inner strength and moved on more
peacefully to being me or gone inwards, become bitter and twisted
and eventually committed suicide. I feel the latter is more likely.
My codependence on my family, mixed with the shame I felt, was
an unbelievably toxic mix. It is as hard as hell to break free from
that kind of thing. I hate it when people say things like, 'all you
have to do is walk away'. That is complete bollocks! One might as
well have an invisible bungee cord strapped around one's waist. In
codependent families or relationships there is no separating one
person from the rest of the unit; they are so deeply enmeshed. It is a
horrible state of affairs. Bound together by myriad forms of control
and shame, it takes a determined and concerted effort to break free,
along with the willingness to change at any price and go through an
unbelievable pain barrier. It feels like one is going against every
instinct one has but it is not the truth. The truth is this: for someone

to have their own life, who is currently trapped in this scenario, they have to learn to love themselves, by themselves, for themselves and that is a hard task for one who has been so used to giving away their freedom, power and lives to others.

Codependence is self-sacrifice. It enables us, and those we are in the toxic relationship with, to carry on with our old, bad behaviours. The people we leave behind may never change and we must learn that we can do nothing about this. Guilt ensues and we question whether we are bad for leaving them behind or moving away. No. It is no more than a trick of our ego to think that we can return and change them; that is their job, not ours. The most powerful thing we can do is change ourselves. Change yourself and then watch others around you change too. It happens and when it does it is heart-warming!

A List of Crap Things to Say

Below is list of things that will make you stand out as a raving bell-end to any transgender person you quote this pseudo-spiritual and/or well-meaning nonsense to:

- 'I know how you feel.' No. You don't. You really don't! How on earth could you?
- 'Just be.' Piss off!
- 'You should get a more masculine/feminine haircut.' You cheeky tosser!

- 'I'd love to take you shopping and get you some clothes that make you look more like you should be.' You incredibly cheeky tosser!!
- 'Ignore what others think of you.' Valid but you try it!
- 'You'll be wanting a boyfriend/girlfriend now' (to fit in with my gender concept of you). Why?
- 'You know it will be harder getting a job if you change sex.' What the hell has that got to do with anything? How is getting a job going to make me feel better about myself if I'm in the wrong gender anyway?
- 'Do you ever wonder what God will think of you changing sex.' No and I don't fucking care either!
- 'Sex could be an issue.' Really? You mean more than it is now because I don't have the correct sex organs for my gender? I'm properly screwed now then, aren't I?
- 'How will you get clothes and shoes?' Personally, I have found clothing outlets and shoe shops great for satisfying this requirement.
- 'There is no need to feel ashamed of yourself.' Again, a valid point but the chances are that if one is transgender, this is a default setting. We're brought up with it just because we want to be ourselves.
- 'Don't get angry with people who don't understand you.' Oh, yeah? Why not? How the hell would you feel and don't bloody tell me not to get angry! Arsehole!

- 'I've been thinking about your sex change. If I were you...' Unless you are transgender yourself, stop right there. I detect large quantities of bullshit are to follow!
- 'I can cure you, you know. You can feel comfortable being the same sex you were born with. It is what you are meant to be. The angels and God want it too.' If ever anyone says anything like this to you, run in the opposite direction as fast as you can! People like this are dangerous if you are vulnerable and you could end up in a very big mess or, even worse, taking your own life. I had this said to me some time ago by a minor celeb who professed to be 'at the top of her field', (out of her tree is more like it). Apparently, she could see psychic tendrils coming from me that were trapping me in past lives that I have led as a woman. According to her, it was these past lives I lived, mostly as a woman, that were making me want to change sex, 'mutilate' myself with operations and take hormones. Funny that. I know another well respected psychic that believes I have led many former lives as a man and I tend to go with her for reasons that I will not go into here. Another thing is, this psychic charges a fraction of the cost for a consultation that the minor celeb psychic does! There are some very dangerous people out there; do your own thing at the end of the day. Consult with other transgender people and specialists in this field and forget those who

>have never been there or have some other interest; often ego, money or status.

This list is not exhaustive. There are fools waiting to open their mouths with gems of dubious wisdom everywhere. Just be aware that they are out there and be careful! Above all, watch out for the well meaning crazies too.

The world is full of people with their own agendas. None of us are exempt from this but some of us are more aware than others. Some of us are more honest than others and genuinely want to help more than some, with the added bonus of the humility to realise that, maybe we are wrong.

'Cause Ah's Black, Innit?!

All I did was ask him if he wanted coffee. I might as well have asked him if he wanted a fuck. The look of fear in his eyes was so telling of what was inside his addled brain; 'Oh no, she fancies me!' Well, not really, not at all in fact. I just thought the man was interesting and it would be good to have a chat, get to know him. Maybe not, eh?

The trouble with stereotyping is people really do believe it on quite a deep level. To be transgender means that one is always up for sex, for some unknown reason. Being gay or bisexual, also for some unknown reason, can mean the same thing but being gay or bisexual also means that you are naturally endowed with artistic skills and abilities. It's like being black I guess because, as we all know, black people have natural rhythm, don't they? Yuk! What an awful way to think. Below is a poem I wrote about a situation that arose within a group I used to belong to:

Because Ah's Black

I'm just not included
The role doesn't fit,
And no one quite gets
Why I'm feeling like shit!

I point out the problem
I'm told, 'that's not right',
So why am I left
Feeling like shite?!

Attempts to include me
Are just bouncing back,
Is it because
Maybe ah's black!

Again I get handed
The part second best,
And again it's because
It's the part I do best!

> I guess I don't fit
> What you want me to be,
> And I guess it's because
> You don't want to see.
>
> If I didn't push
> Certain buttons in you,
> I feel you would give me
> My credit, my due.

That, my friends, is exactly what it is all about; pushing people's buttons and leaving them in an awkward place within themselves. From that place creeps their unresolved stuff and where their demons lurk. If one is lucky, they will see what is going on and do something about it. If not, do what I did and leave the group!

A Cure for Prejudice

Jenny, a friend of mine, has given me a rather tall order but one that I shall try to fulfil to the best of my abilities. 'Your diagnosis of prejudice is spot on,' she said, 'can you come up with a cure?' Well, here goes.

The paradox of this matter is thus: It is complex and simple all at the one time! Prejudice has the same qualities as alcoholism, drug or sex addiction. Its symptoms differ and are paradoxically the same. Where it does differ is that prejudice is the drug **and** the disease, another thing making it so hard for the sufferer to see.

Okay, we know all this so what can we do about it?

Multiculturalism is a great way forward if the communities mix and share their lives (or are not afraid to) but what I really feel is of more help than anything is proper, spiritual education because it helps us to understand who we are as individuals, not as a group. When we strip away the ego (no, I'm not saying the ego is bad) and take a look underneath, then we can start to see who we are and our place amongst others. By totally looking at who we are as individuals we can connect to others. The ego is who we are in this world and on this plane. It is our personality, taste and discernment in so many areas. Take that away and we get down to brass tacks, our foundations. Strip us of religion, jobs, social status and all the ideas of who we are, and we are just the same as everyone else because at a fundamental level, all that stuff means very little. It is a means of identity that we have built up in this world, one way or another.

It takes humility to see that we are wrong in our ways because humility is the flip side of ego. Please do not get this confused and think that ego is bad. Humility and ego can work beautifully together if a balance is found and will allow the person to dance through life. Ego is fun, have some!

One thing I can guarantee is, if we show a prejudiced person hatred, we will entrench them more in their ways than if we show them love. It can be difficult to feel kindness towards someone who shows such destructive views, but if we show them anger and disapproval, we are telling them that our views and who we are is more important than their views and who they are. This is the illusion they are fighting against in the first place, don't help them to get further into the trap. If you cannot show love, keep away. The chances are that anyone who is severely prejudiced has not come from a happy background. Prejudiced people are generally not happy, how can they be? They are constantly guarding against attack. They do not live with peace. They may even perceive living with anger as an asset, indeed I have met such people.

Do not ever underestimate the power of love but also, never underestimate the damage one can do by trying to do good if one is coming from a place of judgement. You will just be a mirror image of the person you are supposedly trying to help but are, in fact, prejudging. Anyone see a cycle here?

Come from love or keep away is my solution to prejudice whether it is within ourselves or within others. There you go, Jenny. I hope this is up to the mark.

A Slightly Alternative Look at Prejudice.

Bigotry, racism and prejudice, although quite vile, are interesting subjects. It raises questions such as, 'Where does it come from and how does it start?' 'Is it something that is innate in us as some ancient survival instinct that we no longer need?' I don't actually believe that these 'qualities' are innate in us. As a child, I did not judge others until they did something to me. I was little interested in what others were like regarding being coloured or religious or sexually different and, as a matter of fact, if someone was different, I found it to be interesting and I wanted to know about them. I was not racist or sexist or homophobic but I was taught to be later on in life. These people were a threat or bad because they were black or gay or a religion that was foreign to this country, no other reason. No, I was not born that way and I am wise enough now not to buy into that fear-fuelled rubbish. I used an example of homophobia a few weeks ago, one that always springs to mind and makes me cringe when I think about it. It is from the old 1970s television series, 'Are You Being Served?' The audience used to whoop uncontrollably when Mr Humphries 'did something gay'. I used to watch this as a child and, although too young to understand the implications of it, I understood from the reaction of the audience that Mr Humphries was doing something 'wrong' or against what he 'should' be doing. It was subtle indoctrination, call it what you will but that is what it was, whether intentionally or otherwise. This type of stuff has been around for years and I remember an Enid Blyton book that a friend of mine had. It dated from the fifties or sixties I would guess and was all about the Golliwogs. I also remember the station master in one of Enid's books literally kicking a Golliwog off the platform because it was black. Tell me kids don't pick up from this that black people are 'wrong' and I'll call you a bloody liar. Of course they do! What are they meant to think?

I can remember 'trying to get my own back' on kids at school who had called me names, so I copied what they had done to me and looked at their features or behaviour, trying to find an anomaly in it; something that was uncommon or different. They did it to me so why should I not do it to them? This is the start of prejudice; finding something about the person that is different but harmless, shaming them in front of others because of it, making an issue out of something that is quite human and perfectly okay.

The process is simple:

- Feel completely inadequate about oneself and therefore angry.
- Find an attribute in another, uncommon to others around them.
- Shame that person and spread rumours about them because of that attribute.

The cycle is self-perpetuating. This is prejudice in all its cunning, horrible glory. It is a disease and is therefore alive. A disease needs to feed or it will die and it must have a way of reproducing. Clever isn't it? Quite a few people have trouble around accepting emotional or spiritual imbalance as a disease, as 'disease' is mainly looked upon as a medical and physical malady but the patterns are the same and the end result is the same. Disease unchecked runs riot and causes havoc, so do negative emotions and spiritual imbalances.

Prejudice thrives on shame and anger. All diseases need a host to feed from; a food supply. Prejudice needs shame and anger to exist. It is a smart disease because it is aware that once it has started to grow, it is going to need more and more food, just like a cancer spreading through the body, but should it be recognised for what it is, it will be destroyed. Like many cancers, one cannot see it until it has really gotten a hold. It is only later that the signs show and the pains start.

To survive in the host, prejudice must be seen to protect itself and the host with righteous anger; a good thing, it tries to make one believe. It has to keep to the shaming of others ritual and vehemently guard against being shamed itself. This, of course, is totally impossible and a reproductive tactic of prejudice. If I see flaws in you, then I must see flaws in myself.

Now this is the really clever part, the con trick of prejudice. Here it sits in its host, quietly growing away unnoticed and all the time it has its food supply all sorted out with vast quantities of anger and shame. It is very much apart from, not a part of, the healthy spiritual humans we can be, as it has disguised itself as a protection mechanism while all the time feeding off our negative emotions.

Here is how the disease spreads and rapidly reproduces:

- Prejudice of another.
- Creates anger through fear of that person.

- Creates shame in ourself should we be found to be like that person in any way.
- Creates anger through fear of that situation occurring.
- Creates shame at the thought of the situation exposing us as vulnerable.
- Creates prejudice.

The cycle speeds up, as with most diseases, the more advanced it becomes. Do you see the pattern? In a few seconds it has reproduced itself and given the sufferer a shot in the arm with more prejudice! Some call it reinforcing beliefs but either way the disease has doubled its fortifications and dug in for a fight. Entrenched prejudice is as hard as hell to get rid of if the sufferer cannot recognise it and that is why I have written this to help people see the malady for the con trick that it is.

The Gender Trap

The gender trap is a trap that we all fall into at one time or another. In fact, most of us live our lives by it. To the many, it is a code by which we live and breathe because we know no better and it is a way of life that is hard to break free from.
The more rigid we are regarding who we are as male or female, the harder our lives are. It dictates to us what clothes we wear, what

movies and programmes we should watch and even how we should behave.

So, how has this come about? I feel that this sort of social control, and that is exactly what it is, has its origins in male religions. It does not serve to benefit the male species and in fact hinders them greatly, as it does females. This separation of the genders is also used by big business and the media. Why? Because it sells stuff! Also, people are harder to control if they are connected by a common bond. None of us are all male or all female although many or most of us are predominantly male or female but we think we are one or the other.

It is thousands of years of careful indoctrination by those in power and seeking power. So, you ask, how does it work? The answer is simple; it weakens people. Those who do not care about whether they are male or female are much stronger people because they do not have the internal struggle and conflict that others have. They do not limit themselves. They are open to possibilities that others are not. They are free to have relationships with whom they please. They do not have to prove themselves like others do. They are content with who they are at a fundamental level.

Another sad fact is that it is not only the straight people who are caught in this charade; there is a significant part of the lesbian, gay, bisexual and transgender communities too. One would have thought we would have got our act together and recognised this long ago but no, we are still bitching at each other's sense of dress, sexual habits and even criticising the way each other walks, talks and sits! Geez! Breathtaking shit or what? These ignorant views we have of what we should be doing, behaving like, thinking, wearing, liking is fathoms deep but needs to stop or we will destroy ourselves. I'm not a conspiracy theorist and I don't think that certain people are 'doing this to us' intentionally, well maybe some are but I just believe that we are all caught up in lies about who we are and it is aiding our downfall. Ego, greed, bigotry and pride are a nasty combo but they are what is behind our ignorance. This ignorance is fuelling consumerism, keeping people poor, destroying our planet and making us very unhappy.

World economy does not thrive on contentment. The economy, as we know it, is a monster that loves conflict, struggle and constantly needs to be fed. The more we give it, the more it needs. It thrives on the gender lies that we live. It knows that to live up to the unrealistic expectation of our sense of masculinity and femininity we have to spend a lot of money; we cannot relax and just be. It thrives on shame, the threat of violence and bullying if we cannot be like the emaciated female models or the muscle-bound, tanned men in adverts and magazines. What will the neighbours and our friends say if we can't afford a new car? It thrives on our fears of rejection and inadequacy. It cannot let us be, because *it* needs to be. The answer is simple. If you do not want such a monster to live, cut off its food supply. This is simple enough to do if you are willing to accept yourself for who you are and love yourself in the moment, now.

Doing The Best We Can

Try to remember one thing on a daily basis: At any given moment, we are all doing the best we can with what we have got. It is our lifelong experience that brings us to any moment in time. This gives us the right to criticise and be criticised. Without this knowledge, we lose the luxury of discourse and dialogue. Without discussion we lack the ability to progress as human beings. Never forget that we are ALL doing the best we can at any given moment. This does not mean that we cannot improve ourselves in the future and the above can also be a trap where we fall into our egos, using it as an excuse to ignore the tools we have, or not search for others. Discussion with humility is the way forward, I find. I try to argue with the feeling that I am right in what I believe but also leave the possibility that I may be incorrect. That way the ego, a fundamental and useful part of being human, is kept in check.

What is the ego? I suppose it is our concept of reality which is ultimately a very personal viewpoint and can vary greatly depending on how we feel about ourselves and the world around us. Never underestimate its uses! It is a valuable tool and I don't believe it is a good thing to batter it to death as it is a part of us. Dispensing of the ego is an ego trip in itself. None of us are all spiritual. If we think we are, then our ego has run away with itself and we are dangerously unaware.

To use as a tool, the ego is great for having fun with life as we can reinvent ourselves and also fire our imaginations using it. It can be a way to reshape our reality in this world. It becomes negative when we lose ourselves in it, imagining that we are better than or worse than others and have more or less of a place in the world than we actually have. Yes, thinking that we are less than, is an ego trip too! This is how the term 'going to the shrink to have one's head shrunk' came about. No one's head is in fact shrunk, it is just the ego that the experts attempt to take down to size! A bit of a paradox if we think we are less than others but no, it is still valid to shrink the ego in this case. I also want to bring to attention just how 'less than' and 'more than' are perceived in society. 'More than' is seen as being big headed but being 'less than' can actually be seen as an attribute and it is so not. Nothing could be further from the truth. It is a false state of being that, like its counterpart, carries a story that we buy into on a daily basis.

Interesting how we associate the ego with the head, isn't it? The ego is, I believe, a tool of the brain and affected by chemical and electrical processes. I am not saying that it cannot be affected spiritually; of course it can. Ego then, is an Earthly tool of the mind but spiritual matters seem to come from the heart chakra and are linked every bit as much to our physical state, albeit in a different way.

The ego does not tell us how things actually are; it puts them in a context that we can use to process things from a personal point of view. This is why spirituality is so important. The ego is ever-changing and spirituality is a constant. Using the two in conjunction with each other is invaluable because it keeps balance.

Also, used in conjunction with each other, they provide a 'dance'. This dance can be very grounding, allows the user to see another's point of view and can also be highly creative.

Show me an artist, an inventor or any creative person that does not work largely with their ego. The time where spirituality mixed with ego becomes useful is when dealing with our mundane lives and the lives of others. If we remember that we are no better or worse than anyone else, that we are all doing the best that we can at any given time and all of our experiences have brought us to this point, then we shall do well by ourselves and by others.

Inner Conflict

I am writing this piece after a storm. It is impossible to tell what damage has been caused by a storm when one is in it. Only afterwards is there a clear and safe place to take a look around at what has happened and attempt to clear up the mess.

I am still trying to pick up the pieces of my life and piece them together. Some people think we correct our gender and all is well. I'm years on into this and still working at who I am. Okay, I am a lot more together and sorted than I ever was but the life and lie that I led did a humungous amount of damage and takes a lot of unravelling. The real me comes out when I feel safe enough to be me.

I posted on Facebook in a discussion on mental health that I have PTSD (Post Traumatic Stress Disorder). Mention this condition and most people get the picture that you were in a war zone. In a way I was but it was an internal one with myself. Conflict rages on the back of fear.

My PTSD took on a lot of the signs of someone who had been in a war zone. I suffered from rage, alienation, guilt, shame and suicidal thoughts. It is a miracle that I am still alive today considering the poor mental state I was in. Why was I in such a state? Purely because I was denying my sexuality and my gender orientation or, more correctly, didn't feel safe enough to explore who I was. That's a hell of a price to pay, don't you think? Well, I feel in some ways I am lucky because I made it to the other side. We may never know how many transgender people don't make it though.

I hate to think how many transgender people couldn't come out, internalised all their feelings and then went on to commit suicide. Believe me, when you're in that place, it is a very tempting opt-out choice.

Often, people say to me how brave I was to come out and be myself. Isn't it sad that in this day and age it is seen as brave to be yourself? Geez, what a world! The truth of the matter is that I wasn't brave, I just got to a point in my life where it was too painful not to be me, whatever the consequences. Bravery is not even in the equation and when I 'came out' back in 2004 I didn't really have a foggy clue who I was. I wasn't going to tell that to anyone though; I've had too many people wanting to pigeon-hole me, stick labels on me and fix me for no other reason than to feel more comfortable with themselves, although none of them would ever admit to this or be able to see it.

I am a brave person in many ways but how does one 'come out' if one doesn't know who one is? There is now a 'Q' at the end of LGBT. For the less well informed this means Lesbian, Gay, Bisexual, Transgender and 'Questioning'. When I was growing up, there was no Q allowed. 'What the fuck are you talking about, you must know who you are!' would have been a typical neanderthal, dim-shit response to sexual exploration where I came from or any self-exploration come to that.

'Who am I?' was not an invitation to an existential debate, it was more an invitation for a punch in the head. I was among fuckwits and learned to behave like one to survive. Not everyone around me was like this but the ones I seemed to be stuck with, who were very influential in my life, were, and I couldn't seem to escape either.

The Committing Of Sin

No make-up for this face today
that eczema has so ravaged,
So fear creeps in to wear me thin
Will I get verbally savaged?

Are the clothes I wear too butch? I ask
Are my boots too masculine?
Somewhere, deep, inside myself
I fear I'm committing sin!

I shouldn't look at women now
I feel it's just not right,
What happened to just being me?
I really talk some shite!

Faint heart has never won fair maid
And I really must confess;
I've pulled some gorgeous totty
Since I put on a dress!

This is a good example of shame and how we are all doomed to get it wrong, whatever our gender status. No one can live up to the stereotype expectations on a daily basis that are thrust at us in magazines and on television.
A hero of mine, Bruce Lee, once said; 'I was not put on Earth to live up to your expectations and you were not put on earth to live up to mine.' How profound and how freeing! The message is, I believe; 'Be yourself, nothing else matters.' When this is accomplished, I do not feel the need to bend others to my will or bend to that of others. Life, and everyone in my life, is good enough; there is no need to change anything, only to seek out those

I need to be with and things I need to be doing, and in some cases just to be is all I need.

Sexual Shame

Help a person discover their gender and sexuality and you can help free that person. Discover the power that gender and sexuality have, create a belief system or religion that shames sexual joy and pleasure and you can rule the world. I cling to no religion or faith label anymore. I have used such labels as Christian or Pagan, which suited my spiritual path better, latterly but no more.

I did not realise it, but shame kept me going around in circles for a long time; years in fact. If it is shameful to have certain desires or pleasures there is the possibility for denial of those pleasures, to convince oneself that these pleasures are not needed or not real. Sexual desires are, in my view, more of a need than a desire. Not to fulfil or pursue them is like putting a dam across a river; keep building up the dam and you may be able to take the pressure but all of your time and energy will be taken building up that dam. What a waste of time and energy!

If everybody spent their time pursuing something worthwhile like discovering who they are, their sexual and gender orientations, their creativity, mass social control like that of the church and oppressive governments would be impossible. No one would be interested in the crazy fantasies of the few megalomaniacs. Who would care? Well, look around at what has become of us; most of us care about the rantings of the deluded few. We vote them in, follow their teachings and go against what we need on a regular basis.

There are two powers in the universe: one which creates and one which destroys. One is love and joy and the other is sickness and destruction. I was too sick at one time, spiritually, emotionally and physically, to be able to make any real choices. To discover who I was I needed a sense of self and that had been well and truly taken from me. The needs of others had come first; their feelings, thoughts, lives and their ideas about how I should live my life. I am a giver, but now I only give to those who really deserve my attention. Those who took from me were very needy but there are some needs that no other human being can fulfil; I didn't know that or I would have saved myself so much time and pain.

If someone or something is not serving my journey, I let them go. I need to be free to be me. I do not have the strength any more to live a lie; it is too tiring. I am unbendingly loyal to those who love me unconditionally, why should I not be? They are my supporters and rock in an uncertain ocean where, without their help, I would have drowned a long time ago.

Going To The Toilet

Have you ever walked into a pub or restaurant and tried to avoid having a pee, going to the toilet, call it what you will? If so, is it because you have a strong aversion to using public loos or is it because of the sound your pee might make going into the toilet? 'What?' you ask. Why would that be an issue?

Okay, look at it this way. A man peeing into a toilet bowl sounds like he is trying to bore a hole in the porcelain. Sitting down is much the same, especially if the pressure is a bit high. Sitting down and peeing onto the bowl above the waterline is not a good move either if the pressure is high as one can get unwanted splash-back. Now, men and women pee differently, that much I know and I'm not talking about the difference in body parts. What I mean is the way it comes out. As mentioned before, men pee as if boring a hole in the porcelain but women tend to make a gushing sound akin to a small waterfall in a stream.

Why on earth should I notice such a thing? Well, because I am a transgender female but still pre-operative. This means that if I go to the ladies' toilet I can end up making a sound as if I'm boring a hole in the porcelain. The other reason is previous bullying and a wish never to get shamed around such stuff. The lengths I have been to, to make my pee sound like every other woman's pee. I have it down to a bit of an art now. I pee into the water, at the waterline and this makes a gushing sound. I still get paranoid that some pervy woman is going to look under the door to see which way my feet are facing! I could sit down and apply the same tactics but it is a public toilet and one is never sure who has used it previously. It takes time to line the seat with loo roll too and one doesn't always have time. By God, I still have a few of the fears, don't I? I'm not surprised; I have faced a lot of prejudice. I have this ongoing and hard to shift fear that when I go to the toilet in a public place there is going to be some bigot of a woman who, listening to the sound of my pee, says something like, 'There's a man in these toilets! I want him out!' It is not a likely scenario nor is it true from experience as far as I am concerned but it is a fear I have. It is also highly unlikely to happen as the woman would sound like a complete perv trying to explain it to the bar staff; 'Well, I was standing there, listening to someone peeing when I realised that the sound was not what I expected!' No shit, really?

Small-Mindedness

Small-mindedness – a lack of thought and disregard of another's point of view. Not looking at the wider picture. Judgement without experience or limited experience of a person or subject.
There are other definitions that I also find to be helpful and informative. If I am being small-minded, I am discontent and disconnected to spirit. I am lacking connection to others and to who I am. That is small-mindedness for me.
We can all do it, be that way, at some time or another. For some, it is a way of life that they do not break free from. I use the term 'break free' because when I am small-minded I am in a trap, self-focused and usually angry or fearful about something. As a rule, I can spot it fairly quickly and break the chains. It has taken a lot of awareness though.

As I say, we can all be small-minded. I respect anyone who admits to it because it not something that most people would gladly lay claim to being, on anything other than a short term basis. Any decent spiritual teacher will admit to not being perfect and having small-minded thoughts at times.

It is a sort of defence mechanism: 'If I don't like them because they are (black, white, gay, poor, rich or for whatever reason), I will not let them into my life and therefore I cannot get hurt'. This is a strategy that on the surface seems okay if we let it go quickly afterwards but soon becomes a disease, especially if it is internalised instead of voiced and no one can challenge it. There is always something hidden underneath that is the real cause of this discomfort.

I have been known to damn half of the world population by saying that all men are violent. Really? Of course they are not! I know loads that aren't. What that statement is covering up is past abuse from certain men; not the entire population, but just to be sure, I will block out the chance of getting hurt again by a man and this I do by condemning them all. That is small-minded. Being small-minded keeps me small and restricts my choices. It limits where I go and with whom I communicate.

Vulnerability is the antidote to small-mindedness. Vulnerability opens doors because it is another version of humility. Vulnerability is an admission and acceptance of reality. Don't get vulnerability confused with letting people in so that they can walk all over you; that's stupidity and a lack of boundaries.

I can sense when I have let someone in that is potentially not good for me. I can feel my aura close down to them. It is like a door shutting. I have learned more and more to listen to this sensation as it is a saviour. Now, when I am vulnerable, I can filter people this way, I don't have to make generalisations about people to protect myself. When I have prejudged someone in the past, and it has happened not that long ago, I am in danger of alienating them without knowing what they are like, without letting them close enough to feel what they are like and, who knows, not getting to know someone who could be a great friend or colleague. That is the rub, the trap.

Small-mindedness is prejudice, plain and simple. We prejudge something or someone without experiencing what it or they are like in reality. This is my point; reality is what is in our minds at any given time. That is what we experience. If we buy into the fear, we are maybe buying into an illusion, who knows? We don't know because we are not willing to get close enough to find out for ourselves. The assumption has been made, a conclusion has been reached and that is the reality as we perceive it. Look at it like this and it's scary, isn't it?

Body Shame

My little cat sits in the empty bath tub, gazing lovingly into my eyes as I sit naked on the toilet and nip off a number two. Izzy is completely unaware that if God sees this, the world will end and the baby Jesus will never stop crying. She knows nothing of this and cares not about my bodily function or the fact that I have no clothes on. She is only concerned with making contact with me and getting/giving some love. She knows not body-shame, because she has never been taught it. No one should be taught body-shame but it has become part of our culture to teach each other that our bodies are bad, need to be covered up, should or shouldn't have hair and should be a certain shape otherwise we will be abused. That is the long and short of it; if we do not conform, we will be abused. The authorities, religion and our peers have taught us this, and to expect this.

I was very lucky when I was growing up in the fact that I was never made to feel ashamed of my body. This was probably one of the few but main things that saved me from going completely over the edge as, being transgender, I was not comfortable with my body. Nevertheless, I was not ashamed of it either. I did know that many people viewed being naked as a sin and that God's eyes would drop out and his nipples invert if someone did get seen naked in a public place but I find it to be a ludicrous view.

I picked up a lot of society's crap when my denial broke about myself and I changed gender. I didn't want to pick up the lies out there but fell into the trap anyway. It was fear. I was different, felt it and was made to feel it by every crap-head and ne'r-do-well out there. So, I shaved everything and stuck lots of make-up on, whether I wanted to or not. How messed up was that? This was the point at which shame crept in for me. 'Uncomfortable' is the central heating a bit too high. 'Shame' is one's home on fire!

Why all this shame about our bodies? We all have one and they are all different. Not one of us looks the same as another person. Also, what is all this crap about body hair? Why do some women feel they have to shave all the hair of their vaginas to look like pre-pubescent girls? Why do men feel they have to grow the stuff like self-cultivating farmers? The whole thing is a sad, unhealthy joke.

I seldom shave my body hair. Being a transgender woman, one would think that sort of thing would be a priority for me, would one not? Let's turn that around. Why would one think that a priority for me? Oh, I see, to fit in. Well, here is the news; I never want to fit in with that sort of crap. The other reason is, most of the time I just can't be bothered.

If you are really concerned and hung up about body hair and personal grooming don't worry because you have already been well groomed – by society, the media and religion. Yep, 'your ass is theirs', as they say in the States. (Well, as long as you've shaved it properly!)

If you have a partner that does not like your body hair, shape or other stuff about it then you have the wrong partner for you. Do yourself a favour and end the relationship. If that person desperately wants to cling onto the relationship, even though they obviously do not like aspects of your body, it might be a good idea to get rid of them. At best, they are seriously codependent. At worst, they are going to be highly abusive to you. Who, in a healthy state of mind, has an intimate relationship with someone they do not fancy? No one.

Being in love, properly in love is about accepting the other person the way they are and loving them, warts and all as we say. True love is not banished by a tuft of hair (or lack of it) under one's armpit.

Male & Female – What Are They?

There seems to be much confusion and fixed ideas on what is feminine and what is masculine. There are baseline views which assume that anyone with a penis is male and anyone with a vagina is female. These are not views from the great thinkers of our times but more common than one may know. If only it were that simple but in many ways, thank God it isn't; there would be absolutely no diversity of any kind.

Some people's concept of what is masculine is severely skewed to the point that they think anger is a masculine trait and a positive quality! Shocking but true; I've met them. This means that any woman who counts herself as truly female is not allowed to get angry. I smell danger here!

Let us start to break this all down to find out what the true nature of male/masculine and female/feminine actually are. We all have similar traits. Women get 'broody' and want kids. So do some men. We look upon motherly women as maternal and fatherly men as paternal but is it not all the same energy?

The need to protect a loved one, be it a child, a friend, a pet or a partner. Is that masculine or feminine energy? Do most men and women not possess this quality?

Does what we wear make us male or female, masculine or feminine? Not from my findings. I have known some pretty butch and tough men that like dressing up in women's clothes. I've also known quite a few women that would have made a far better job of being a man than I ever could have done if aggression and lack of sensitivity are male qualities. Also, what is between one's legs is irrelevant to what one's gender is.

I fully believe that male and female are no more or less than 'ego roles'. Again, please do not dismiss the ego as unimportant, or bad, as sadly some do. It is a vital piece of our Earthly character that helps us function in this world. Also, the ego I believe, is a mirror of our soul needs, what we need to be in this life to progress further as beings, to helps us learn more. A lot of what we perceive ourselves to be is, in fact, an illusion. How often have we proved ourselves to be wrong about an aspect of ourselves? What we sometimes hold dear as an undisputed fact can sometimes be a complete lie or misinterpretation of a truth.

I have known straight, feminine men and straight, masculine women whom I would not class as having matching, biological genders but they seem happy with who they are. I know gay men that, as far as I am concerned, are undisputedly male and the same with lesbian women who are undisputedly female. My findings are, that it is all strictly down to the ego, spiritual needs and how we are most comfortable playing our role in this world, that makes us male or female, nothing else.

More of the Mystery Unravels!

A few years ago, a friend said to me that they could see my ideal partner being a dark-haired, alternative life-styled and quite masculine lesbian. I just nodded, knowing that to contradict would mean a discussion and explanation which I sorely wanted to avoid. No, I really cannot see me ending my days in front of a log burner in a remote location with a T-shirt and combats-wearing lesbian, knitting Tibetan rugs out of pubic hairs. It's just not my bag!
I love women but I am into the more feminine ones. I do like some men too but the energy of women is more attractive to me. Saying that, due to some of my life experiences with men in the past, I have been more than a little shut off from them, so in reality, it is bloody hard to tell for certain what my feelings are about men from a sexual relationship point of view to begin with.
From the start, I saw men as a threat and, after suffering every form of abuse possible at the hands of my so-called best friend and, also at the age of thirteen, getting 'fisted' by a male doctor in my local surgery whilst going through the agonies of a suspected appendicitis, I have been more than a little cautious about developing close relationships with any of them. I wondered why that doctor wanted my mum to stay outside the room while he

'examined' me. What a bastard! Never let your child be examined alone by anyone, no matter what excuse you are given.

I did not stop being attracted to men but later on in life, when I really started to figure out what I was all about, something shut down in me. I stopped looking at men in any way, shape or form. I secretly hated them and didn't think I should be fancying women. I was in a right old pickle. Mad as a hatter and terrified of telling anyone.

More and more as I discover who I am, I realise that I am attracted to both sexes and opening up to men again. Not all men and women are the same. I have always thought though, that if I were to have a relationship with a man, it would have to be an open one because I could not live with the thought of not having another sexual relationship with a woman. It comes as a shock to me to find that all my ideals about me being monogamous are maybe a pile of nonsense but, at the same time, it is a relief. Maybe I thought that 'Monogamy' was that time of the year after Christmas when everyone gets pissed.

Looking at the above and after considering it all, I do still think that it is possible for me to settle down with 'the right woman.' I see the benefits and beauty of working at relationships. There is so much to gain by sticking by each other as long as the love hasn't gone. That is the key factor in it all.

So, who is my ideal partner? I'll know them when I see them but I'm up for fun in the meantime!

Seeking Refuge

I have a vision of a world where there is no need to 'come out', where people just dress the way they want to, take hormones, have gender correction ops and nobody thinks anything of it but I feel that is a long way off, not even in my lifetime. In the meantime, while we are hopefully getting there, I would love it if there were a retreat for transgender people to go to at the start of their coming out. A sort of community where it was possible to stay for a considerable period of time to help the most vulnerable ones get their life on track.

What I am talking about is a place that would help people who were in the situation I

was in and the not so severe cases too. I hate to think that there are people out there going through what I went through; it's inhuman. How reliant I was on other people and the approval and validation I needed, the shame, the self-hate and levels of entrenched self-sabotage and denial is beyond belief. It takes a long time to rehabilitate someone with these kinds of complex needs.

A community where people could come and stay for a reasonable length of time is my vision until we evolve more as a species and can let others just be without a need to harm them. A place where people could get together for group-work and much needed therapies. A place where people could be, share their experiences, support one another and not live in fear of 'being different' at their most vulnerable stage in transition.

For all those politicians, doctors, department of work and pension people who reckon it is so easy just to change gender and support oneself, I would love to set them a task. I would, literally, make them cut their hair in a fashion that left their forehead bare. In the middle of their forehead I would get a very clever make-up artist to put a very convincing false eye. They would have to go around with this for six months in a place where they were not known and could not reveal their identity.

I wonder how completely fucked their self esteem and mental health would be after that? I wonder how blasé they would be about sending vulnerable people out into the work place then.

If any of you think this is too extreme and doesn't represent what I went through you are so wrong. This is exactly what I went through. Let us look at how people would treat such an alien image as someone with an eye in the middle of their forehead and how they would cope. They would be met with the following severe prejudice:

- Unable to make friends easily.
- People gossiping about them constantly.
- Insults in the street.
- Threats of violence.
- Physical attacks, nearly always by men (or so called men).
- Stared at.
- Driven out of where they live.
- Difficulty getting and keeping employment.

- General, ongoing low and high level abuse.

These are just a few of the delights awaiting someone on this mission! What they are unlikely to encounter are rejection by family and friends, who will know that they in fact do not have a third eye in their forehead, and they will also be able to see an end to it, (I have been relatively lucky and escaped the physical attacks since changing gender. I also have a loving mother and supportive relatives, mainly on my mother's side, plus a good bunch of friends I can rely on, but many do not). Is this an unrealistic comparison? Not in the least. It is highly accurate. Anyone arguing that the difference lies in that I made a choice and they didn't, have not been listening: I had no choice and I didn't want to be transgender! DO YOU UNDERSTAND? I have never liked being transgender although it has its gifts. I would love to know what it is like to inhabit a fully functional, biologically female body. I felt terrible shame and self hatred around being me, exactly as if some twat had stuck a third eye in the middle of my forehead.

Now do you get it? To those that say, 'rejoice in who and what you are', sometimes I'd like to reply, 'Piss off you complete and utter bell-end because you obviously don't quite get it and think you are so bloody knowledgable.'

It is good to rejoice in who we are but only if we truly feel like rejoicing, because sometimes, being who we are sucks and blows!

OUR History!

History. His-story. Yes, the old history tomes were generally written by men. There is much more modern history written by women, which is a good thing and provides balance but what of the transgender community? We are lacking, badly.

It is hardly surprising to learn that many of us just want to change sex and live 'normal' lives, whatever guise that may take, but the truth is that there are few of us who 'pass' as being completely biological male or females, no matter what surgery or treatments we have undergone. Also, what a horrible term 'pass' is! Pass as what exactly? Aren't we all just members of the human race and should we not rejoice and embrace our differences?

Transgender history is manyfold if one knows how and where to look. Joan of Arc refused to dress as a woman, boys that went on to become members of the church were known as 'being put into skirts'. I wonder how many men and boys joined the church because they wished to dress in female attire? I know that it was one of the reasons I joined and became an altar boy. Yes, I was looking for something spiritual but this was a huge factor in my decision. We are there but disguised because of the sin factor or shame factor as I regard it. Nevertheless, we are there! There are many times past in which I have decried the media but they have brought us 'out' a bit in various ways. Okay, not always in a positive light but out into the light at any rate.

The Shamans of old were known to dress in the opposite attire to their gender as, it is believed, this helped them to walk between the worlds. I remember an incident that happened to me at a Druid camp I went to shortly after starting my hormone treatment. I was pre-op and made no secret of it. The camp was Beltane and for this occasion the camp was split into two groups; male and female. There was a women's lodge and a men's lodge. I was asked if I would like to be one of the walkers between the worlds as I hadn't had the op and could act as a messenger between the camps. I was most uncomfortable with this and said 'no, absolutely not'. I had not come this far and suffered so much to walk between the bloody worlds!

A discussion was held and it was decided that I would be allowed into the women's lodge. I was relieved and a little bemused that this discussion had taken place at all. Had I not been allowed in I would have packed up my tent and gone home. I had always seen Paganism as a way to free myself of stereotypes and still do. There are however, and there will always be I imagine, people in all walks of life and all areas who perpetuate these rules for whatever reason they have. I can't say too much about rules as I tend to be a rule maker as well but they tend to keep me stuck and are often highly unproductive.

It would be great if more of us embraced being transgender and celebrated our lives as this is how it should be. I don't have any problem with those who 'pass' and just want to remain anonymous; that is their journey and God knows it is their right and I respect them for it. Nor do I have any problem with those who do not pass well but just want to take a back seat and stay quiet; they have probably had enough and simply want to get on with life. Again, God knows, I understand it! Life can be bloody hard for us.

Maybe one day there will be no 'Mr, Mrs or Miss'. People will stop using daft references such as 'Sir or Madam' and we will talk in first name terms and accept that if someone is called Katie or Dave that Katie does not have to have a stereotypical female voice and Dave doesn't have to sound like a typical bloke.

I love some of those questionnaires and forms to fill in: Male or Female. We are all a mix of both. The correct terminology would be: Predominantly Male or Predominantly Female. I wonder how many people could answer that question truthfully from a place of self knowledge? I wonder how many people really know?

The Shop

"You used to work behind the till,
I remember you well there."
I've never worked in any shop
Which till, when and where?

"Of course you did, I know you well
We always had a crack."
Oh, I get the picture now
You know me 'cause Ah's black!

"That shop in town, the one up there,
You served in there a lot."
The girl that served you was TS
And so like me, yeah, NOT!!

5'6" with short fair hair
And make-up wore a'plenty,
I'd just hit forty and two years
And she had just hit thirty.

"Ah, I know you from the Horse and Hound
You do the cabaret act."
This dude has lost the flaming plot
Now ain't that just a fact.

Well, I'm not the girl in the sodding shop
Or the drag queen in that boozer,
I look like me and only me
Piss off you bloody loser!!

The above poem is a good example of prejudice perpetrated by someone who means absolutely no harm but is totally unaware of what they are doing and saying. This is why I use the line, 'You know me 'cause Ah's black': a form of prejudice used against coloured people to denote that they all look the same even when they clearly don't. It's putting people in a box, whether we admit it or not. It's saying that the person is different from us, separate to us. I'm guilty of it myself from time to time.

There are a few transgender people in our community and if someone knows them, they immediately assume that I am connected with them or, more shockingly, I am them!

I know a lot of transgender people, male and female, and not one of them looks remotely like another and people still get confused. It's sad but that's disguised prejudice and the perpetrators don't even have a clue they are doing it.

A good friend of mine once said, 'Oh, you and two other transgender friends went out together on new year's eve? Wow, that must have been such a laugh!'

Why? Would it have been any less funny if my friends had been biologically female or male? You have to see it, hear it and experience this kind of crap to really appreciate just how awful and ignorant it is. Bless you my friend; you didn't mean it, I know.

Being Different

A letter to a local newspaper

A friend told me the other day that I was the odd one out. I thought for a moment and then I said, 'Is it because I'm a non-vegetarian Pagan, because I'm transgender or is it because I still like Phil Collins?' 'No', came the reply, 'It's because you don't have a telly.'

Yes folks, it's true. I don't have a telly! I find them to be time wasters and a dangerous mix of wholesome information with rubbish thrown in and large helpings of fear-based, negative nonsense (aka The News).

My friend argued, 'What if a great world event took place? How would you know?' Well, I guess I'd find out one way or another and if I didn't, I wouldn't care because I wouldn't know. Maybe someone with a telly would let me know.

My friend also argued, 'What if a foreign army were about to march on our shores? Wouldn't you want to know? Where would you be without your telly then?'

Where would I be with one and what good would it do me? Am I supposed to use it against the invaders? Maybe I could take it down to the beach and throw it at the soldiers as they come ashore. I'd favour a small, portable job if that's the case, one with sharp edges on it that would leave a nasty scar.

'What if you get ill?' they said. My reply was, 'I'd read, write, get creative, talk to family and friends.' That's pretty much what I do anyway.

There is also the radio. I love listening to the radio. Again, it's another way to find out if invading armies are breaching our defences (it's also smaller than a telly and much easier to throw at invading soldiers). I do use selective hearing even with the radio, especially when I hear a sentence beginning with the words, 'Scientists are saying.' God save us from what the scientists are saying!

Anyway, I digress. My point is, I'm different because I don't have a telly. Great, suits me!

Too Shy?

Shyness is not a commodity valued in our society. That is a pity. It has so much to offer. I have found depth, recovery, sexuality, sensuality, privacy, space to be, reflectiveness, observation and the space to be me.

Why is this not valued? Why the struggle? I can only feel that it is the growing obsession with consumerism. Run faster, buy bigger and still know who we are! Not possible. It is a Pandora's box. We can only go so far into this abyss before we crack. Then we are lost. I know this, I got lost. God knows I ran. I was a shy child and it was not a quality that was valued. My playmate was an extrovert girl down the road and my father always used to say to me; 'why can't you be more like her?'. The simple reason I couldn't be like her was because I was myself. No one should be asked to make an exchange like that, no one, I don't care who they are or what they are going to turn out like. We all have a valid place in this world. No one learns from the perfect being, how can they?

In shyness lies humility, personal secrets, the edge of discovery, huge emotional potential waiting to be released, sexiness, vulnerability (another misinterpreted state of being), resolve and that coiled spring that is the soul waiting to emerge! Never underestimate shy; you will be missing out on so much.

I hated my shyness. I perceived it as a weakness and therefore I struggled with it, tried to defeat it and inevitably caused myself great pain by pushing through it. Of course, I never really pushed through it, just did things I felt quintessentially uncomfortable with. I made a complete tit of myself just to prove I could be one of the boys, out there and having fun. Centre stage, unless a shy person is ready for it, and I MEAN READY, is not a good place to be. It traumatises the shy person, switches them off to their feelings (how else could a shy person exist in such an environment) and causes extreme stress. Sexual performance goes through the floorboards, paranoia creeps in (what DO people think of me?) and, if the person is as trapped as I was and can see no way out, the cycle continues. It's hell! If one is trying to live up to the expectations that I was, madness ensues, and it did.

Shyness is not something to conquer; it is something to revel in, enjoy for its qualities and edge out of very slowly, depending on how sensitive one is. Don't hate it, love it! God, what I'd give for the world not to know some of the things about me that it does. Revealing oneself to the world when we are ready is one of the most powerful things we can do for ourselves and for those around us to witness. That's power! That's the way to really show others what we've got!

Assumptions

Assumptions are another thing that people make along with crazy statements that make one's jaw drop. Here are some below:

'You'll be wanting a boyfriend now that you have changed sex.'
Why would I suddenly want a boyfriend? I have altered my biological body, not had a brain transplant. I am bisexual and always have been, though in various states of denial, trying hard to be either a man or a woman as I thought I should be through the eyes of society and all its stereotypes.

'So, you were born a man then.'
No, I was just a baby when I was born (from my mother's point of view, I am very glad about this fact).

(Many years ago, just after my name change.)
'You'll obviously wait until after all the operations before having sex with anyone.'
Why would I wait? What is so wrong with me the way I was/am? If people don't want me for a partner for any such reasons, then they are the wrong people for me anyway.

'You look a lot better in that outfit today.'
Geez, thanks friend. Was I looking crap before (in your opinion)?

(This one got back to me a couple of years ago. To clarify, this was meant in a sexual context.)

'Katie's transgender. She'll have been all 'round the place!'

Why would my sex drive be any different to anyone else's? I am way less promiscuous than a lot of people I know. Sleeping around just doesn't do it for me; I crave intimacy.

'Transvestites are different from transexuals because transvestites get a sexual kick from dressing up.'

I get a sexual kick from dressing up, so do many men and women and that is just from dressing within their own gender. It is natural to have sexual feelings like this. This is 'your sexuality'. Enjoy it, don't push it away and be ashamed!

(A conversation at work one day.)

Colleague – I always dress up for work and then dress in something different at home.

Me – So do I. I really enjoy dressing up though.

Colleague – Well, you would, wouldn't you? Dressing up I mean (followed by nervous chuckle).

Question: Why would I enjoy dressing up any more than anyone else?

'Oh, you've got a job.'

No shit Sherlock... Another common assumption made about me is that I am either well off or quite poor. This can also mean, 'We didn't think anyone would employ someone like you.' Yeah, well I've got some fucking news for you!

<u>LGBT Wot?!!</u>

I don't want to be L,G or B
And I really hate label T,
I'm Katie today
And I'm not straight or gay
Do you get my point, don't you see?!

Everybody alive craves a label
Every Dick, every Joe, every Mabel,
They keep the straights straight
And the gay people gay
And enlightenment under the table!

And it's labels that's given us kinks
By the righteous, the moral, the finks,
When our natural's wrong
How we feel don't belong
That kind of thinking just stinks!

Now, if we should all be the same
If we all shared one common name,
If sex didn't matter

And names didn't flatter
Our egos or cause ourselves shame.

Life would be so much less complex
If we weren't so obsessed with our sex,
Let us shag how we want
And our dress sense to flaunt
On impulse rather than reflex!

I've no sides for attaching a handle
To fuel a great torch or a candle,
I relinquish the tags
And drop all those bags
Label me? Not a chance, fuckin' scandal!

Below, is a letter to a national paper. I didn't keep the article itself, sorry. Also, I don't know if this ever got printed.

Dear Editor,

Re: Feminism Is Still A Great Word - G2; 06/03/2012

I read Annie Lennox's article with enthusiasm and encouragement. What perception! Feminism needs to be seen and, more importantly, better understood. I really believe that its bad press and reputation comes from the fact that even many of the feminist movement just do not understand its meaning, qualities and, therefore go against the fundamental ideals of what it stands for. Feminism as I see it is totally inclusive. It embraces men and women whether straight, gay, bisexual or transgender. It stands for dignity, compassion, nurture, values our natural environment, emotional intelligence, empathy and spiritual strength. Feminism is the balance against the rigid structures of a patriarchal society and male dominated religions.

Both masculine and feminine energies/qualities exist in us all; it would be impossible to live as functional human beings without this mix. In a predominantly patriarchal society, greed and 'might over right' has tended to be the way for too long. We desperately need to find and redress the balance.

Is it ironic that so many gay men have shunned the feminist movement or could this be to do with feeling excluded by some of its prejudiced female members? I really feel this to be the case. There is much prejudice towards gay men and transgender women from the lesbian feminist community. Is it not also ironic that so many lesbian women who shun transgender women as 'not real women' have more than their fair share of masculine energy and male looks? The time has come, methinks, to put this foolishness aside and move forward to inclusion not apartheid; a negative quality heartily shouted down and protested against by feminist activists.

Feminism has so much to offer the world. It could take us away from some of the ignorance of religion and male dominance to teach us who we are as people, not how we are meant to think, feel, dress, who we should sleep with etc...or is this one of the other reasons it gets bad press? How much freedom do the patriarchs want us to have?

Whatever our own opinions are, the world we live in is changing and a lot of the positive change that has evolved over the last century or so has feminist qualities written all over it; equal pay, gay and mixed marriages, votes for women, equality in the work place, rights for animals and the bill of human rights to name but a few. We need to keep going.

Feminism is not just a great word, it is a great way for the world to move forward.

Drummer Statue, Truro

A letter to the local paper;

Dear Editor,

Re article; 'Drummer Is Obscene'.

I find it so sad that anyone can perceive the naked human body as obscene. If this is so then a newly born baby would be obscene instead of a miracle. Sex would also be an obscene act instead of a beautiful union between two people. To look upon ourselves naked would be what; shameful, obscene, a sin?

I have come across such views about the naked human form before and can only conclude that anyone holding such views must carry a lot of misplaced anger and repressed feelings. I wouldn't like to even hint at what those feelings may or may not be.

This letter is not intended to shame the writer of the article but to educate. The human body is not obscene, our sex organs are not obscene but they will become so if those are the labels we choose to put on them.

I have to admit I think the statue could have been better finished but maybe I've missed something. Whatever, well done to the artist! Keep breaking those stupid, unnecessary taboos.

I Had A Dream…

I needed not husband or wife
I loved me and so loved my life,
I became as life ambled
Without safety gambled
As I feared not a fist or a knife.

I dressed how I wished without dread
And enjoyed every stitch, every thread,
When I spoke I'd not pale
Fear my voice was too male
Being me was plenty street cred.

> I cared little the gait of my walk
> Or if someone was spotting my cock,
> The hairs on my arms
> Were just added charms
> Let's face it; there's miles on the clock!

> Oh, the joy of just living free
> Not L or G or B T,
> To live how I please
> And the moment to seize
> With you all, and us and yes, me.

Jesus Wept!

A letter to the local paper;

Dear Editor,

I have followed the discourse between Pagan and Christian parties in your columns recently with more than a little sadness in my heart at what I am reading.
Would it not be great if we could just even TRY to tolerate one another's beliefs without lecturing on what we believe to be right or wrong? At the end of the day, that is exactly what it is; our own beliefs. Mr X, no one knows the will of God, and Jesus certainly

wouldn't have stood for bigotry against homosexuals as far as I can make out, or against anyone for that matter.

The saying 'Jesus wept' springs to mind at the moment. If he were among us now and saw the way that some of us behave in his name I'm sure it would sadden him greatly. Hearing Pagans miscall Christians doesn't exactly fill me with glee either.

I am a Pagan who was once a member of the Church of England. I can remember times as a Christian when I made remarks against Paganism. Since I converted to Paganism there have been times in the past when I have made remarks against Christianity. I have since come to realise that whatever faith I belong to, it is unjust to condemn other people for their beliefs. Love begets love, fear and hatred beget fear and hatred. I think my Christian girlfriend would agree with that!

Dying For Our Beliefs

Light around me
And light within,
To shine in this world
Is not a sin!

Fear not to live,
Fear not to die,
Religion is
The biggest lie!

Stories written
By the dour,
Misogynist bigots
Craving power.

Hefty tomes
Turn lives to tombs
To control the masses
And fill the wombs.

So long ago
In forgotten lands
Devils made work
For idle hands!

Hall of Mirrors

Look deep into the mirrors, pray
Take note of what you see,
'Cause all you see that's in me
Is what you see in thee!

Feast your eyes awhile in thought
I am your mirror dark,
Spread tale and gossip far and wide
It's about you too, pray hark!

> You are the demon of your words
> The one you love and hate,
> Adjust your view in the mirror, now
> As *you* reveal *your* fate!

Questions

From time to time I am asked questions. Naturally enough, people are curious and who can blame them but some of the questions are just incredible. Here are some 'face-palm' examples:

Q). You must know what it is like to think like a man and a woman. What are the main differences?
A). I have never known what it is like to think like a man. I have only ever just played a part, taken on male roles just like an actor. How would I know what it is like to think like a man, my brain is predominantly female.

Q). Why do you always wear skirts? Most women don't wear skirts every day.
A). I had more than thirty years of enforced trouser-wearing. I'm a little sick of the fucking things. Also, I find skirts to be a lot more feminine attire than trousers, less boring, more fun to dress up in, and sexier. Yes, it is the 21st century, women are allowed to be sexy. We all are; men too. Just allow yourself to enjoy yourself.

Q). Why don't you try wearing make-up? Don't you like it?
A). As a matter of fact, I love make-up but have you seen the shitty rashes I get on my face and round my eyes? Try putting make-up on that and see how it looks.

Q). How do you have sex? Like, if you have a girlfriend, which you have. People ask these things you know?
A). Sadly, I do know. Haven't you ever heard of making love? Are the mechanics of my sex life *that* fascinating? If it is, fuck off. Go voyeur someone else's ass!

Cornwall Pride

A letter to the local paper:

I attended Cornwall Pride in Truro on Saturday 25th August 2011. What a great atmosphere! I used to shy away from Pride events simply because I just wanted to get on with my life and not bother about what my gender or sexual identity was. As time went on I began to realise just how important it is to stand up and be counted and say 'NO' to prejudice of any kind and to celebrate who we are as individuals and as a group.
Carrying the LGBTQ (Lesbian, Gay, Bisexual, Trans or Questioning) flag through the streets felt fantastic; I was lucky enough to be near the front. It was also great to see support from those in the shops as we passed, many giving a wave and a smile.

Martin Luther King had a dream of equality for black people and I have a similar dream for LGBTQs. My dream is that one day there will be no need to 'come out', we will just be in love with someone. My dream is that one day there will be no LGBTQ community because we will all just be human beings getting along together, accepting and rejoicing in each other's differences. My dream is that one day there will not be a threat of violence when someone wishes to express their love for another of the same gender or because we wear different clothing to what others think we should wear. My dream is that one day people will not suffer fear and hatred at the hands of others because they are considered to be too male or female for their gender. It is my dream, that one day we will all know who we are, because we will all be allowed to be who we are.

The End

Thank you for reading my book!

If you have any thoughts or feelings about it, please use the links below and share them with others:

https://www.facebook.com/flowersandtightropes

https://twitter.com/

http://www.amazon.co.uk/

http://www.goodreads.com/

Also, if you feel inspired to write your own book and need professional coaching like I did, look here:

http://anjakersten.com/

for Anja Kersten's web page and contact details. *Good luck!*

Please visit my website to find out where and when I will be giving talks on my book and about my life experiences:

http://www.samphira.co.uk/